D0119535

This book provides an introductory survey of current research on English language—its grammar, sound and spelling systems, and vocabulary. It focuses on the aspects of current linguistics studies which are most applicable to the teaching of English. Chapters 3—5 show how traditional and transformational grammar are related and what contribution each makes to language teaching • Chapter 6 examines the question of why grammar should be taught at all • Chapters 7 and 8 show the relation between the English sound and spelling systems and show what rules determine the spelling of non-phonetically spelled words • Chapter 10 discusses the question of what kind of language to teach in the light of the regional, social, and stylistic variations which characterize modern English.

FRED BRENGELMAN, Ph.D. University of Washington, is Professor of Linguistics, Fresno State College.

The English Language

The English Language

AN INTRODUCTION FOR TEACHERS

Fred Brengelman
Fresno State College

Prentice-Hall, Inc. Englewood Cliffs, N. J.

PRENTICE-HALL INTERNATIONAL, INC., *London*
PRENTICE-HALL OF AUSTRALIA, PTY., LTD., *Sydney*
PRENTICE-HALL OF CANADA, LTD., *Toronto*
PRENTICE-HALL OF INDIA PRIVATE LIMITED, *New Delhi*
PRENTICE-HALL OF JAPAN, INC., *Tokyo*

To Mary

Preface

This book is an introductory survey of current findings about the English language. It focuses on the aspects of current linguistics research which in the author's judgment have the clearest application to the teaching of English. The topics it examines have been under discussion for some time and form a solid part of the developing body of knowledge about the English language, particularly as related to the traditional responsibilities of the language arts teacher.

The book is not restricted to one approach to the study of English, nor does it reflect the views of any one of the groups engaged in the current controversy about what direction transformational-generative grammar should take. On the contrary, the book is intended to provide an overview of some currently developing areas of English language study without abandoning valuable insights from traditional and structural linguistics. It seeks to provide a transition from the unordered, usage-focused school grammar that most teachers are familiar with to a more systematic kind of language study. By exposing the reader to the idea of generative grammar and to some current theories of phonology, semantics, and style, the book hopes to bridge the gap between the grammatical tradition and the radically new approach to grammar which has grown out of the work of Noam Chomsky. It attempts to express key ideas from modern grammatical theory in terms already familiar to the language arts teacher.

The first two chapters give a short introduction to language and language study. Chapters 3–6 present a rudimentary outline of generative grammar in a format similar to that which the teacher is likely to meet in some currently available school materials. The main purpose of these chapters is to clarify the concept of transformational-generative grammar rather than to present a fully-developed theory. The rules presented here will be familiar to anyone with a background in traditional and structural grammar. Only the format is different. There is no attempt to argue for a specific set of rules constituting the "deep" grammar of English—and presumably all languages—but rather to show how generative operations can be expressed, and to illuminate some features of English grammar which are a necessary concern of the language arts teacher.

The second purpose of Chapters 3–6 is to suggest some of the uses to which grammar may be put in lower-school teaching. The author's view is that new grammatical constructions can be mastered best through the use of teaching materials based on the best grammatical theory. Materials for teaching English as a foreign language, for teaching new social class dialects, and for teaching new styles all must be based in part on a grammatical analysis of English. The insights of generative grammar seem on their face to provide a better basis for the teaching of sentence construction than those of the school tradition. An adequate grammar is also central to certain levels of literary interpretation and to the understanding of other aspects of social behavior.

Chapters 7 and 8 describe in traditional terms the phonemic and graphic systems of English. The concept of the phoneme is used here because the author believes that the English spelling system can be described best with reference to a segmented representation. These chapters suggest the general outlines of a spelling and reading program which makes maximum use of the regularities underlying our spelling system.

Chapter 9 deals with the definition of the word and with the notion of definition. It draws on current discussion of the idea of meaning features and on the notion of the lexicon as providing a full statement of both the semantic and grammatical co-occurrence privileges of words.

Chapter 10 is a discussion of regional, social, stylistic, and historical variation in English. It considers how language change takes place, what features of English are most likely to vary, and what a well-informed attitude toward language change might be.

It is hoped that the topics for investigation and the reading materials suggested throughout the text will promote and facilitate further research and study.

This book has grown out of the author's experience as a teacher of linguistics in N.D.E.A. English Institutes. The author is indebted to the institute participants for providing the set of questions that this book attempts to answer, and for their lively and critical evaluations of his answers.

Table of Contents

The English Language

Introduction

CHAPTER 1 The importance of language in human affairs has been recognized since the beginnings of literature and history. All of what our tradition tells us are distinctive human characteristics are related to language: reason, conscience, the will—however these may be defined—are names for the internalizing of dialogues learned in language exchange with other human beings. The manipulation of abstractions and the preservation of general principles, without which the human achievements in art, technology, and philosophy would have been impossible, can exist only as language. All the major religions attribute to the use of language in the repetition of sacred texts the power to save or destroy. In baptismal rituals it is usually held that the water could not perform the miracle of spiritual cleansing without the words. And this ancient recognition of the peculiarly humanizing role of language has made the deliberate teaching of language part of education almost from its beginnings. This teaching has included such practical topics as rhetoric and logic, those language skills that win arguments; and it has included such impractical ones as attempts to fix and refine natural languages through prescriptive teaching. It has also included the teaching of archaic or obsolescent language forms for liturgical and ceremonial purposes, as in churches and courts of law. In any case, the acquisition of the command of language has for thousands of years claimed a very large percentage of educators' time and attention. And despite the geometrical increase in the quantity of information about the physical world, the average student's time is still devoted primarily to learning to handle language, beginning with reading and writing and continuing through rhetoric and literary analysis. These studies almost invariably make use of statements about the phonological, lexical, and grammatical structure of English.

Naturally enough, studies with a long history tend to develop a traditional subject matter with accompanying formulae of presentation. The rhetorical terminology of the ancient Greeks survives to the present as the only generally recognized apparatus of the rhetorician. Similarly, not only the terminology but the assumptions and methods of ancient Greek and Roman phoneticians and grammarians dominate the language study of the

1

132184

schools. The study of sounds is commonly still the study of letters, with such terms as "long" and "short" and "diphthong," all of ancient origin, introduced (sometimes quite inaccurately) to relate a writing system invented for one language to the sound system of another. School grammar, "modern" or otherwise, still faithfully devotes large amounts of time to one of the admittedly great contributions of the classical grammarians, identifying parts of speech, despite the fact that this emphasis often obscures other significant facts about language. The existence of a tradition such as the one described here makes the task of the teacher particularly complicated. On the one hand, the tradition is part of the general culture; it is part of the body of knowledge that is presupposed by writers and thinkers. On the other hand, the tradition may act as a straitjacket, discouraging research or making it difficult to apply the results of research to the teaching of important subjects. A classical instance of the effect of such a tradition in the history of another science is the trauma which western European scholarship experienced following the discoveries of Copernicus and Galileo. These discoveries required a major adjustment not only for astronomers but also for the general public, priest and layman, affecting sermons and folk sayings, and ultimately the foundations of their faith. We must hasten to say that no similar catastrophic advances appear to have been made in the field of linguistics. It is true that researches by linguists during the last two hundred years have demonstrated the evolutionary origin of languages, the regularity of sound change, and the existence of a high degree of system and structure in language. They have exploded myths about the so-called primitive languages, and they have found better ways to describe familiar languages. But revolutionary breakthroughs have not taken place. It has, however, been the case with English teaching that not even the relatively modest new insights have had much effect on school materials, partly because teachers regard them as destructive to a valued tradition.

Among these insights, perhaps the most important is the point of view toward language and the study of language that has become general because of the success of recent linguistic research. Language has been demonstrated to be the kind of phenomenon that is open to various kinds of scientific investigation. That is, language is in some sense a constant, something that can be looked at steadily and objectively like the other constants of human social behavior which anthropologists and sociologists have learned how to investigate. It is possible to collect data and make generalizations about both the current state of a language and its earlier history. This current attitude is characterized by objectivity, by a willingness to look at language data as all equally interesting from the theoretical point of view. Thus, for example, language change is not viewed necessarily as evidence of decay or progress; and "lower class" social dialects can no longer be viewed as degenerate forms of some "standard" dialect. This is not to say that prescriptive statements about language have been or ought to be discarded. It is, rather, to say that such statements can now have a much firmer empirical basis: terms which used to cover the language teacher's whims, such as "provincial," "illiterate," "slang," "archaic," or "vulgar" can be defined; and empirical investigation can show how particular language forms ought to be classified. The complicated language structures of extended discourse are still largely uninvestigated, but a beginning has been made in the description of at least those language forms which represent a competence shared by the general mass of the speakers of a given language or dialect.

Current research into language can be divided, somewhat loosely, into, first, those studies relating language to extralinguistic facts, such as studies of usage, stylistics, dialectology (both regional and social), acoustic and articulatory phonetics, and the psychology of language. A second group of studies are more purely linguistic (although, of course, all language study must take human social behavior as its basic set of data); these include phonological and grammatical analysis undertaken with a view to providing models or schemata that will account for all normal utterances in a given language. Both these groups of studies are typically synchronic: that is, they deal with a language at a given point in its history. A third branch of linguistic research, historical linguistics, may be classed separately from the two groups mentioned above because of its focus on language change. It may be concerned with the variations of grammatical rules or with the migrations of peoples, or both; but it stands by itself because of its attempt to account for language variation in time. These approaches to the study of language will be discussed further in the next chapter.

Not all of these studies are equally relevant to teaching; indeed, some of them (such as the development of mathematical models of language) are so new that their basic procedures are still being worked out. Some, such as dialectology, have been developing for a long time, and have well-established procedures and large bodies of findings, often of great significance for language teaching. Others, such as transformational grammar, are relatively new but sufficiently developed to shed significant light on topics language teachers deal with. The chapters that follow will attempt to show, in a brief and elementary way, some of the recent findings of linguists which provide insights into the English language and the ways it may be studied.

The Study of Language

CHAPTER 2 Because language is at the same time an independent signaling system and a reflection of human thought and culture, because it appears to be fully developed at any given time but is in a state of constant change, because it has both literal and allusive functions, the study of language covers a wide range of topics, and any one topic can be approached in different ways.

Perhaps the first decision that must be made by the language researcher who is interested in applying the results of his study to teaching is whether to approach the subject as a law-giver or as a law-inferrer. That is, he must decide whether he is going to impose rules based on external considerations or whether he is going to infer rules from data. People preparing school materials seldom deliberately make up rules of language; it is completely impractical, as everyone knows, to apply such an approach wholesale except to an artificial auxiliary language like Esperanto. But when it is asserted that a double negative construction should be avoided because it is illogical or that "ain't" is vulgar or that the "shall" and "will" rules make a valuable distinction in meaning, then rules are being imposed, not inferred. That is, purported descriptions of a language which base their rules on logic or prestige or any consideration other than grammar common to native speakers of the language are giving, not inferring, laws. The vast majority of school grammars and a great many dictionaries still in print give evidence that judgments of taste or "correctness" have affected their content, resulting in the omission or proscription of language forms actually in general use by speakers of English. Needless to say, when rules have no basis in the actual practice of native speakers, they have little chance of shedding light on a language. The most serious objection to an approach to language study based on considerations other than the practice of the native speaker, however, is the fact that such study runs the risk of failing to discover important and pervasive generalizations about the history and current state of a language. It necessarily reflects the value system of its practitioner (for example, he may simply prefer eighteenth-century English, he may admire analogy, or he may dislike borrowed forms). Such an approach has always been considered absurd in other fields of inquiry, and it is equally absurd in

4

language study. Despite widely held opinion to the contrary, language study is fundamentally unlike theology, which assumes an external absolute revealed in authoritative texts. Dictionaries and grammars are not like Bibles. A statement about a language must be evaluated in the same way as any statement in the sciences—is it accurate? is it explicit? does it account for all the data? is it economical? does it form part of a coherent theory? And every student of language has as his primary task the revising, supplementing, and replacing of the existing statements about his subject.

For a time, all prescriptive grammar, whatever its basis, was regarded by scholars as a kind of antigrammar, a threat to the genuine scientific study of language. It need not be this, of course. A grammar for a foreign learner or a dictionary for a native speaker trying to improve his command of his own language is necessarily prescriptive but not necessarily false. It is only when prescriptive grammar is based on irrelevant considerations such as what "sounds good," what is most conservative, what is most regular, or the like, that it becomes a threat to legitimate grammar. Prescriptions based on accurate analysis of the language and of the extralinguistic situations to which language relates may have great value. A distinction must be made, of course, between perfectly arbitrary prescriptions and prescriptions based on stylistic analysis or on considerations of class and region. It is a perfectly correct observation that "ain't" is not used (although it may be mentioned) in serious written English and that "I want out" and "couldn't nobody" are regional, not general English. It is arbitrary, however, to insist on "whom" as an introductory word in questions or to require "I should like" instead of "I would like."

Thus an important question which every student of language must decide is whether he wants to study language as a subject in itself or whether he wants to study it in relation to something else. He could, for example, study language in relation to history, showing how historical events such as conquests or cultural diffusion are reflected in language. He could study it in relation to the value system or the dissection of reality of a given society; he thus could make observations about the relation of kinship terminology to the concept of the family or the relation of terms that might be translated "courage," "honor," or "pride" to the approved behavior of members of the society. He could study language in relation to literary art, noting the different impressions particular uses of language such as metaphor, grammatical class shift, word order distortion, or stress pattern may produce. If, on the other hand, he chooses to study language as a subject in itself, he still has some choices to make. He must decide in the first place what he thinks language is. There are some notions about language that he would surely abandon after a little research; for example, he might start with the assumption that human language is like that of bees or dolphins—a communication system which comes to him fully developed as part of his genetic makeup, not learned, and essentially the same for all members of the species.

Or he might assume that there is a necessary connection between language symbols and the things they signify. That is, he might assume that slime is called by that name because "slime" sounds slimy, or that bulls are so called because of the way they act. A little research will show that not much of any language can be accounted for in this way. But there are harder decisions to make: for example, how much of language can be reduced to a systematic statement? The answer to this question involves many smaller decisions: does each language use an arbitrary list of sounds, or do the sounds form some sort of scheme whereby a relatively few distinctive features are combined in orderly ways to produce the different words of the language? Is each sentence unique, or are all the sentences composed according to a given set of patterns? Is the vocabulary arbitrary, or does it also reflect an underlying system, perhaps of semantic features?

But perhaps the hardest question of all is how much of human communicative behavior constitutes language. Surely not all human noises are the same sort of thing. Because laughing and crying, for example, do not seem to fit into sentences in the way that nouns and verbs do, the student will almost certainly exclude them from his discussion of language. But what about the range of intonation contours—our ways of signaling anger, suspicion, contempt, and the like at the same time that we are uttering ordinary sentences? And what about the gestures that accompany language, often obligatorily, and which seem to differ from society to society in the same way that other language habits do? And he must answer a closely related question: are all utterances to be taken as equally typical instances of the use of language, or are some more representative than others? For example, is a sentence like Hopkins' "Leaves, like the things of man, you with your fresh thought care for, can you?" to form the basis for a statement about English grammatical patterns? Somehow, the researcher must separate the false starts, the poetic distortions, the lapses of the tongue from the utterances which can form the basis for a usable description of the language. If he is a native speaker, this will usually be fairly easy to do. He will at least be able to classify some utterances as categorically grammatical and others as categorically ungrammatical. If he is not, he must rely on the judgments of native speakers.

And besides all this the researcher must be aware that language varies from occasion to occasion, region to region, social class to social class, and from style to style. He may choose to deal only with those features of language which he believes are common to all of these situations, limiting his study to basic grammar and vocabulary. If he wishes to go beyond these aspects of language, he must carefully define the situation from which he is drawing data. Written English, of course, involves a graphic symbolism which can be explained best in relation to the spoken English it represents. But there are sentence types, words, and grammatical constructions which occur almost exclusively in either spoken or written English but not both. All language description beyond the "basic" level is the description of a dialect or style. The heavy emphasis in the schools on "educated" written English should not obscure the fact that all the varieties of English have developed to serve their users' needs, and the linguist cannot consider any variant better or more interesting in an absolute sense.

This study deals for the most part with the English language itself and will not attempt to apply facts about language to other subjects. It will be concerned with the language at a given point in its history, the present. It will assume that our language is highly systematic—in other words, that our apparently infinitely varied sentences are put together according to a finite set of rules applying to all aspects of language, most obviously to sounds, least obviously to words. It will be concerned with what we assume are normal, direct instances of the language. That is, it will draw on our experience of millions of sentences to reject those that contain unique or nearly unique lapses or errors, or that are distorted for jocular, poetic, or rhetorical purposes. It will be concerned with the "grammatical" sentences which native speakers accept as normal, as put together in a familiar and natural way. It will use data consisting of actual utterances by native speakers, particularly when it deals with a special dialect or style, but a description of a language can never be limited to these data, since it is an attempt to uncover the rules for the construction of sentences not yet imagined as well as those attested in data. We will be our own best informants because we can test the acceptability of new constructions based on rules we have derived; and we can get other native speakers to do the same. But in most instances our rules will be at best well-supported hypotheses, since neither we nor our informants will be able to create more than a small part of the total number of sentences which can he produced by following the rules of even a partial grammar.

Like any other kind of study, language study involves description and explanation—reducing masses of data to some kind of order, into a system of classes, for example, and trying to account for their structure or behavior in terms of general principles. Linguistics can be compared to biology, a science which seeks, among other things, to classify living creatures and to explain the system of classes in genetic terms. Similarly, linguistics seeks to identify units, to find what generalizations can apply to more than one unit, and to explain in terms of pervasive rules how the classes that result from these generalizations relate to each other.

Ordinary language provides names for the most important units of language study: words, phrases, sentences, sounds, paragraphs. We have been told about the marvelous powers of words for so long that we may think of language as a collection of words. But words alone or in random strings communicate little or nothing, as an experiment combining in a string, say, the first words on every third page of a dictionary will demonstrate. Our ordinary definition of *word* is rough and ready, leaving much uncertainty about whether compounds like *vacuum cleaner* or constructions containing certain "prefixes" and "suffixes" like *anti* and *'s* (as in "antiwar profiteering" or "the king of England's hat") are several words, one word, or less than a word. Our ordinary definitions of the terms for other language units are equally inexplicit—they correctly identify some important classes, but they do not provide the degree of explicitness that rigorous study may require. For example, our notion of how many "sounds" English has is usually strongly influenced by our spelling, so that we may not notice the rather marked differences between the "t's" of *top, mountain,* and *water;* and we may be uncertain whether "tch" stands for one sound, or two, or three. The term *sentence* is undoubtedly the hardest to define of our common linguistic terms. None of the common criteria such as "having a subject and predicate" or "expressing a complete thought" will account for our intuitive acceptance of "He didn't" as a sentence, though its thought is incomplete, or of one-word answers to questions as sentences, though they lack subject, predicate or both.

The units of linguistic study must include these terms, however, as well as others not so commonly used. In the first place, it seems reasonable to think of any utterance, that is, any actual statement, or question, or request, or reply, as being made up of acoustical phenomena; that is, as physical events that can be measured in terms of frequency and intensity. But only some features of these sounds are relevant to any given language; for example, the aspiration, or puff of breath, that characterizes the "p" in *pin* but not in *spin* is not used to distinguish one word from another in English, but it is so used in Hindi and many other languages. Sound features combine to make larger units—syllables—which are meaningless sound combinations characterized by features of stress, tone, and duration. The smallest meaningful units of language, in the sense that they have definitions, are morphemes, which may be readily recognizable in the form of prefixes, suffixes, or simple bases such as *pre-, -able,* or *boy.* A morpheme need not have any representation at all, as in the case of a word like *cut,* which is a combination of two morphemes *past* and *cut* in the sentence "John cut the bread." That is, *cut* takes zero, or $\varnothing$, as its past tense marker. Words, the next highest unit, consist of one or more morphemes. They may be used separately or in combination to make phrases. The highest unit in most grammatical study is the sentence, a structure that may consist of one phrase or several, and may even contain subordinated sentences. But there are certainly language units larger than the sentence, somewhat crudely accounted for by our traditional definitions of the paragraph. These larger structures are little studied, and our tradional definitions are the best we have at the moment.

Just as words are put together according to rules governing the combination of sound features, so all utterances above the level of words are the result of the application of rules. Indeed, no random combination of morphemes or words can be expected to communicate unambiguously. Even though all the units other than the sound features and the syllables have meanings—sometimes many, sometimes few—which of the possible meanings of a morpheme or phrase may be intended can only be determined after that unit is combined with others in ways which are expected in a given speech community. Not only does the observance of rules of arrangement resolve ambiguity, it also introduces a whole new system of meanings into an utterance. An elaborate system of relations like those of subject, object, modification, cause, condition, prior reference, and numerous others are signaled by arrangement. The fact that we accept both "Running down the street, the boy soon caught up" and "The boy running down the street is my brother" but not "Running down the street, the boy is my brother" (because in the last the position of the "-ing" phrase makes it temporal or causal and therefore meaningless as a modifier of "be my brother") illustrates the intricate way in which arrangement conveys meaning.

The study of a language, then, must be first of all an account of how sentences are put together. This study provides the basis for several of the secondary studies mentioned above: for the study of the relation of sounds to letters and of intonation to punctuation; for the study of rhyme and stress in poetry; for the study of the special effects obtained by deviation from the fundamental patterns of the language; and for the study of all the relations that hold between language and personality, social class, region, and occasion. Linguistics contributes to this very wide area a theory of the construction of sentences.

Topics for Investigation

1. Compare the rules for the use of "who" and "whom," "shall" and "will," the split infinitive, and the double negative in several school textbooks. What justifications are given for observing these rules? What do the justifications imply about the authors' views of the relation of social class and style (e.g., written vs. spoken English) to "correctness" in language?

2. How many rules do you use to make up an ordinary sentence in English? Make up a sentence of about ten words and try to determine how many rules you had to use (mostly without knowing you were doing so). Consider rules covering the arrangement of classes of words and rules covering the changing forms of words to show tense, number, and the like. How many of these rules were mentioned in the grammar you learned in elementary school?

3. A standard language, that is, a language that could be produced and understood equally well by people representing all the geographical areas and social classes of the English-speaking world as well as one all of whose forms would be suited to all occasions, would indeed be desirable. Does such a standard exist at present? What historical conditions lead to stan-

dardization? Are there conditions opposed to it? What should be the attitude of the schools toward language standardization?

4. Compare the prefaces of several collegiate dictionaries. What do they say about their own reliability?

5. What explains the humor in Churchill's famous phrase "up with which I will not put"? Emily Dickinson wrote the lines "A bird came down the walk . . . and then he drank a dew" and "Bring me the sunset in a cup, measure the morning's flagons up, and say how many dew . . ." What special effect does she produce by using count words (*a* and *many*) with "dew"? Hopkins wrote the lines "Nor can foot feel, being shod" and "Nor mouth had, no nor mind, expressed What heart heard of, ghost guessed . . ." Why has he omitted the article before the nouns?

6. Some biologists have compared the "language" of dolphins with human language. Using as your source John Lilly's *Man and Dolphin* (New York: Doubleday & Company, Inc., 1961), consider what justification there seems to be for calling the dolphins' signs a language. Do you see any important differences between dolphin "language" and ours? Consult Karl von Frisch's famous study of the "language" of the bees for information about another elaborate nonhuman signaling system (*Bees: Their Vision, Chemical Senses, and Language* [Ithaca, N. Y.: Cornell University Press, 1950]).

7. Are sounds symbolic? Compose a list of words that strike you as particularly pleasant or unpleasant sounding. Then find other words that are phonetically similar—that are, if possible, different by only one sound feature. Do these words have the same pleasant or unpleasant effects? Is the sound feature by which they differ sufficient to explain the absence of these effects? What besides sound accounts for the attractiveness or unattractiveness of words?

8. Which, if any, of these are instances of the "same" word? How do you decide?

beat and *beet* in spoken English
bear (verb) and *bear* (noun)
to bore (drill holes) and *to bore* (to weary by being dull, long-winded, etc.)

9. Look up the word *air* in your dictionary and compare the compounds beginning with that word. Can you determine what principles explain the use of hyphens, space, and no space in writing these compounds? How satisfactory is the definition of "word" as "a speech sound or series of them having meaning and used as a unit of language"?

10. While native speakers are obviously obeying rules when they make up sentences, they are frequently at a loss to explain what rules they have

used or why they have used them. What accounts for their uncertainty? What implication does your answer have for the teaching of language?

Suggestions for Further Reading

For a brief discussion of the development of linguistics from the sixteenth through the nineteenth centuries see Albert C. Baugh, *A History of the English Language* (New York: Appleton-Century-Crofts, 1957), particularly Chapter 9. Other brief studies may be found in Karl W. Dykema, "Where Our Grammar Came From," *College English*, XXII (April, 1961), 455–65, and in James B. McMillan, "Summary of Nineteenth-Century Historical and Comparative Linguistics," *College Composition and Communication*, V (December, 1954), 140–49. A complete and very interesting account of the emergence of historical linguistics can be found in Holger Pedersen, *The Discovery of Language*, J. W. Spargo, tr. (Bloomington: Indiana University Press, 1962). Leonard Bloomfield's *Language* (New York: Holt Rinehart & Winston, Inc., 1933) is still of major importance to language teachers. While its psychology is now somewhat out of date, its abundant information about the origin and current state of languages around the world and about the phenomena of language change and language variation is unequalled in any other book.

Edward Sapir's *Language* (New York: Harcourt, Brace & World, Inc., 1949) is equally interesting but for quite different reasons. This book raises the key questions every student of language must consider about the nature of his subject and about the way it must be studied.

A book which the reader may find amusing is E. A. Nida's *Linguistic Interludes* (Glendale, Calif.: Summer Institute of Linguistics, 1947), particularly the section entitled "Dr. Zilch and the Golden Age of English."

The Study of Grammar

CHAPTER 3 The grammar of a language is the whole set of rules the speakers of a language use to make up sentences. Thus it includes the rules for making up complex words, like *counter-revolutionary* or *dispute* and for changing the shapes of words to fit into larger grammatical structures, as when a verb like *go* adds *es* after a singular subject. Such rules are often called morphological. It includes the rules for combining words into phrases, phrases into sentences, and sometimes sentences into sentences. Such rules are called syntactic. Morphology and syntax constitute all of what has traditionally been called grammar. The distinction between morphology and syntax seems to have little to defend it except tradition. It is obvious that in English *pretty* is to *prettier* as *beautiful* is to *more beautiful;* that is, that exactly the same process is represented in the first instance by a "morphological" change and in the second by a "syntactic" one. Similarly "my leaving" and "I leave" seem to express the same idea, despite the fact that in the first "I" takes the possessive morpheme while in the second it does not. There is probably something to be said for dealing independently with the structure of certain complex words; but in general no clear boundary can be drawn between morphological and syntactic processes. It has also been recognized in recent years that the sound of a sentence, its phonological shape, is dependent on its morphology and syntax; that is, we do not take a string of spoken words or morphemes and combine them into a sentence. Instead, we form the abstract structure of the sentence and then assign a phonological shape to it. The rules for assigning this shape are also part of the grammar of a sentence. They are called phonological rules.

Grammar is surely one of the most ancient of scholarly disciplines. It was well advanced in Greece and India several centuries before Christ. The pursuit of grammar has, however, been almost exclusively utilitarian until recent times. Panini, the Hindu grammarian, wanted to codify the rules for the makeup of Sanscrit liturgical texts. The ancient Greeks and Romans generally thought of grammar as an adjunct to rhetoric. Indeed, Aristotle in his *Rhetoric* makes the speaking of grammatical Greek the first requirement for success in public speaking. The same sort of motivation still prevails

12

except in highly specialized circles. The teaching of grammar in the schools has been traditionally justified on such grounds as that studying grammar helps students express themselves better, that grammar is a traditional part of the curriculum and requires no further justification, that grammar helps students learn foreign languages better, and the like. The experimental evidence for these claims is slight, but they are not entirely without support. Winston Churchill, for example, attributed his ability as a phrase-maker to the intensive study of theoretical grammar which he was subjected to as a child. Literary critics often rely on the school grammar tradition for the basis and phraseology of their judgments. Learners of foreign languages sometimes remark about how useful their school grammar training has been in helping them master grammatical rules. But these arguments carry little weight when experiments seem to show that students write just as well whether they have had "grammar" or not, new methods of foreign language teaching dispense with rule memorization almost altogether, and traditions are shattered under the onslaught of "modern" approaches to school subjects.

The question whether grammar should form part of the lower school curriculum is not as simple as it sounds. Teaching any subject implies selecting a subject matter and a method. The subject matter of grammar can be theory or skill or both. Skill in grammar can mean skill in avoiding certain grammatical errors or skill in producing effective sentences. A general theory will be the reflection of a philosophy of grammar—and, needless to say, more than one such philosophy exists. As for the methods of teaching grammar, it is clear that grammar is the kind of subject that can be taught deductively or inductively, that it can involve a great deal of practice in sentence construction or none, and that the theory which underlies it (or which forms its exclusive subject matter) may be eclectic or may be the thought of a single grammarian or school of grammarians. Thus when people say that "grammar" has no relation to composition or to interpretation they need to specify what they mean by grammar. We want to consider this subject in greater detail in Chapter VI. But first we need to examine more closely some of the competing theories of grammar.

The choice of a theoretical grammar on which good school materials can be based has been a matter of dispute for a long time. This is true for several reasons. For one thing, the number of grammatical rules needed to explain the construction of any sentence is large. For another, grammatical rules have very complex relations to meaning: the same structure may mean quite different things, as in "a vacuum sweeper" and "a street sweeper"; and the same meaning may be expressed by quite different structures, as in "Seven can sit on that sofa" and "That sofa can seat seven." In addition, a grammar can be approached in quite different ways. From a pragmatic point of view, several approaches may account equally well for the structure of a given sentence or set of sentences; the controversy between grammarians then often focuses not on adequacy but on economy and on clarity. In addition, it is possible to disagree about the relation a grammar should have to the actual processes human beings go through when they make up sentences and when they interpret them. On the one hand, a grammar may be viewed as a model of these processes; on the other, one may disregard these processes entirely and consider a grammar merely a sentence generating or interpreting machine which is adequate if it works. The topic of grammatical theory is obviously tremendously complex; we shall only present some approaches to grammar which appear to complement each other and to illuminate some of the processes by which sentences are constructed and understood. Three kinds of grammars are now familiar, at least by name, to most language arts teachers. These are school grammar, based on a tradition going back to the ancient Greeks which we presumably all learned in the lower grades; structural grammar, which began affecting school materials as long ago as the early fifties; and transformational-generative grammar, which, since the appearance of N. Chomsky's *Syntactic Structures* in 1957, has claimed more and more of the attention of both theoretical and applied linguists. It will be well to begin with school grammar, since it is most familiar and will provide a frame of reference for the discussion of other grammatical approaches.

School grammar is, of course, not really homogeneous, and it differs greatly in complexity from one grammarian to another. It does appear to have some important common features, however. It is ordinarily taught as a framework for prescriptions of the type "*lie* is intransitive; *lay* is transitive" or "subjects of gerunds are in the possessive case," but its main procedure is sentence interpretation. That is, a school-grammar analysis of a sentence is a kind of highly abstract translation of that sentence. The translation consists of identifying words as naming, describing, expressing action, and the like, and of determining their use in given sentences as subjects, predicates, objects, modifiers, and so on. The translation presupposes native command of the language. That is, the analyst must know in advance, though he need not state in his analysis, the structural and contextual signals by which he identifies a word as, for example, a name and not the expression of an action, or as a subject and not an object. Commonly school grammar sets up these categories:

THE EIGHT PARTS OF SPEECH

1. *Nouns:* the names of persons, places, things, and, in some grammars, abstract ideas. Nouns may be singular or plural, and possessive or nonpossessive. (They are sometimes said to have nominative or subjective and objective case, but these categories are neither limited to nouns as such nor applied except as another way of saying that a given construction is a subject, predicate noun, or object.) Certain other constructions filling subject and object positions are also called nouns.

2. *Verbs:* words that express action or being. They have six tenses, including the past, present, and future, and the past perfect, present perfect, and future perfect. Each tense may be progressive, or nonprogressive (i.e., simple). They have two numbers, singular and plural, as well as three persons, first, second, and third. They have two voices, the active and passive. They are also sometimes said to have three moods, indicative, subjunctive, and imperative. Mood is expressed by word order and by auxiliaries, which in school grammar are usually considered a kind of verb.

3. *Adjectives:* words that modify nouns. Some words may be identified as such only in sentences, since the class "adjective" in effect cancels out other class memberships: for example, a noun modifying a noun becomes an adjective. Thus the term "adjective" covers both a class of words and a function of a sentence part. Some subclasses of adjectives are numerals, articles, and possessives, as well as "descriptive" adjectives.

4. *Adverbs:* words that modify verbs, adjectives, or adverbs. Adverbs are identified, in most school grammars, entirely by their relation to other word classes, although they are sometimes said to be words that tell "how," "when," and "where." As in the case of adjectives, members of other classes having this relation are called adverbs. The class obviously contains an assortment of forms with widely different properties: such words as *more, very, eagerly, ten miles, now, indeed,* and *up* may all be called adverbs.

5. *Prepositions:* words that connect nouns to verbs, adjectives, adverbs, or nouns.

6. *Conjunctions:* words that connect structurally similar and semantically "equal" constructions to each other (coordinating conjunctions) or that connect subordinate clauses to the structures to which they are subordinate (subordinating conjunctions).

7. *Pronouns:* words used in place of nouns, including personal pronouns ("I," "he," "they," etc.), indefinite pronouns ("anyone," "something," etc.) and relative and interrogative pronouns ("who," "which," etc.)

8. *Interjections:* grammatically isolated words expressing strong feeling.

The sentence in school grammar is defined as a group of words containing a subject and predicate and expressing a complete thought. Subjects of sentences are topics; predicates are assertions about those topics. Subjects usually contain nouns, although gerunds ("-ing" verbs), infinitives (verbs preceded by "to"), and noun clauses can also be subjects. Predicates always contain verbs. The predicate may contain a direct object (the noun the verb acts on), an indirect object (the receiver of the direct object), a complement (a noun or adjective defining the subject or object), and various kinds of adverbs. Sentences are classified into simple sentences (those having only one subject and one predicate, either of which may be compound and which may have modifiers which do not themselves contain both a subject and a predicate), complex sentences (those having one or more subordinate or included clauses but only one main clause), and compound sentences (those containing two or more main clauses). They are also classified as declarative (giving information), imperative (giving a command), interrogative (asking a question), and exclamatory (expressing strong feeling). Verbs may be converted to participles ("-ing" forms), which modify nouns. Some other terms commonly included are the appositive (an explanatory noun following another noun) and the prepositional phrase (a preposition followed by a noun and usually used as a modifier of nouns and verbs).

School grammars often include a system of diagramming which follows approximately this pattern:

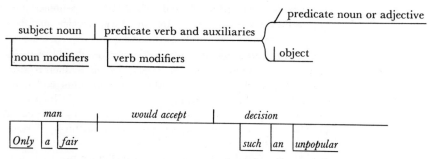

Embedded sentences (subordinate clauses) are diagrammed as sentences and attached by dotted lines to the parts of the main sentence they occupy.

Several things are clear from the above account. First of all, the criteria for classification and the labeling of function are partially, and for some purposes not very happily, combined. That is, the identification of a word in isolation as having the same privileges of occurrence as a given list of other words (e.g., the dictionary labeling of words as nouns, verbs, etc.), which is clearly part of the essential information the speaker uses when he makes up sentences, is not distinguished from the labeling of the function of that word in a given sentence. Thus "vacuum," which is obviously like the nouns "paint" or "air" in important respects, would have to be labeled an adjective in the phrase "vacuum cleaner" according to most school grammar. Similarly, postnominal modifiers such as "selling cars," "tired of war," or "from Spain," which are in both form and meaning members of quite different parts of speech would all have to be considered adjectives under the school definition. It is also clear that the criteria are often rather difficult to apply. For example, the words "one," "none," "themselves," "whoever," "he," "things," and "everybody" all in some sense replace nouns, but only "one" and "he" do so in the sense that a specific noun can be used in their place. Thus in the sequence "I saw some dogs; one was black," "one" replaces "a dog"; and in "Ed came. He was late," "he" replaces "Ed." But "everybody" does not seem to replace any particular noun. Instead, it seems to be used as a cover term for all human nouns, in the same way that "everything" is a cover term for all nonhuman ones. Similar objections can be found to the use of terms like "names," "expressing action," "modification," and the like.

The analysis, further, does not provide a logical basis for constructing sentence production rules, though it is sometimes made to serve that purpose. Thus the same school grammar may say both "A word is an adverb if it modifies a verb, adjective, or adverb" and "In the construction 'He sings good,' 'good' should not be used because it is not an adverb." Thus the grammar seems to presuppose a set of adverbs identified in isolation, such as "well," "happily," and "rather" but not "good" or "happy," despite the fact that the rule suggests that adverbs can be identified only in context. One might also question why precisely this set of categories is set up; why, for example, are so many quite different forms and meanings combined under the heading "adverb"? But, after all these objections are made, it is also clear that school grammar, even as little of it as has been presented here, is a model of language that provides some valuable insights. It sets up a sentence model consisting of phrases headed by nouns and verbs. The nouns and verbs may be expanded by members of other classes which have, in turn, their own expansions. This part of the school grammar model is accepted by almost every grammarian, however radical or iconoclastic. School grammar, however, has defects serious enough to require extensive expansion and modification if anything like a total accounting for the structures of a language is to be made. What it provides is an abstracted semantic structure of sentences, often limited by an arbitrary and constricted technical vocabulary. These defects may be dealt with in various ways, some more successful than others.

The term "structural linguistics," which has occurred in the literature of language teaching for perhaps thirty years, represents one attempt to correct these defects. It is a name given to the kind of grammar done in English by such scholars as Charles C. Fries, W. Nelson Francis, and, in their earliest publications, Paul Roberts and James Sledd. The work of structural linguists is characterized by its attempt to provide a more mechanical and objective means of achieving the goals of school grammar. Following structural principles one can put words into grammatical classes on the basis of their morphology. Words with number inflections are nouns, those with tense inflections are verbs, those inflected for comparison are adjectives, and those with "-ly" are adverbs. This leaves a residue of words which must be classified on the basis of being commutable (i.e., used in the same sentence positions) with nouns, verbs, etc., and which might be called nominals, verbals, and the like, and those not commutable which have to be identified on the basis of their position with regard to nouns, verbs, etc. Thus "boy" is a noun because it can add a suffix signifying plurality; "contain" is a verb because it can add a suffix signifying tense; but "to" is not a verb, noun, adjective, or adverb: it is a member of the class of items that come between, say, "he went" and "town"; "he threw it" and "John." Thus a set of classes can be identified which will provide categories for all the words of the language. But objections must still be raised: are not forms which are structurally unlike in some respects alike in other, equally important ones? Thus while "boy," "diphtheria," "diminution," and "to diminish" are all different both in their inflection and in the function words (words such as *the* and *a*) with which they can occur, they are alike in being able to occur before verbs, with which they can make acceptable simple sentences. It follows, in addition, that merely having a class name for all words in a language, even though the names are arrived at rigorously and objectively, does not provide a basis for stating rules for the production of sentences, a task we can resonably expect a grammar to perform.

Larger structures within the sentence are dealt with in structural grammar by a procedure known as immediate constituent analysis. This is a process similar to school diagramming whereby structures are linked to each other according to the degree of their relationship. (For example, "The" is obviously more closely related to "boy" than to "disappeared" in such a sentence as "The boy disappeared.") An example of an immediate constituent diagram follows:

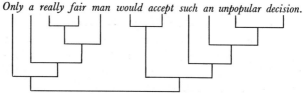

This kind of diagram is somewhat more illuminating than an ordinary school diagram because it can show "nesting" better. Thus "really" modifies "fair"; "really fair" modifies "man"; "a" modifies "really fair man"; and "Only" modifies "a really fair man." This sort of diagram has two defects: its "nodes" are unlabeled, and the diagram is therefore not related to general rules for the production of sentences; and there is no explicit logical justification for diagramming the sentence in just this way. For example, all the linkings are in two's. But perhaps "would" and "such an unpopular decision" are equally closely related to "accept," so that a linking involving three members would have been better. And perhaps "would" relates to the whole phrase "accept such an unpopular decision" rather than to "accept" only. Like school grammar, this kind of grammar does not seem to go far enough toward explaining the structure of sentences.

Transformational-generative grammar is an outgrowth of traditional grammar (on which school grammar is based) and structural grammar. Its principal objective, which gives it its name, is much broader than that of the other grammars just described: it sets out to state the rules that will generate all and only the grammatical sentences of English (i.e., it provides a structural description in terms of a hypothetical sequence of rules). Its conclusions are not limited to what is attested in a corpus of data. It attempts to provide rules that account for not only existing sentences but also all the other sentences that could be produced in a given language at a given time.

Just as a rule of logic such as "If P implies Q and Q is denied, P must be denied" could not be arrived at by collecting large numbers of actual sentences and inferring rules from them, a rule such as "A sentence contains a noun phrase and a verb phrase" must be arrived at by other means than analyzing a collection of speech samples. An examination of actual utterances will not automatically lead the investigator to this rule. Such an examination will show many constructions which lack a noun phrase, a verb phrase, or both. But the NP-VP rule, once it is set up, provides the basis for explaining the grammatical structures of these constructions, just as the logical rule explains the semantics of many different sentences and groups of sentences. There is, of course, a very important difference between a rule of logic and a rule of grammar. The rule of logic has validity because it has a self-evident relation to other rules taken to be self-evident. The validity of a rule of grammar is determined by its ability to account for the way people produce and interpret sentences. The grammarian hopes to formulate rules which correspond to those speakers know and intuitively use when they make up sentences.

Some obvious ways in which transformational-generative grammar is an improvement on earlier grammars are the following: it solves the problems of classification and subclassification which take the form: Should these partially similar constructions be placed in the same class or not? Generally such problems result from failing to recognize that rules are applied to sentences in a certain order and that at one stage in the production of a sentence the focus must be on the similarity but at another on the differences between two forms. For example, in choosing a head-word for a subject, both "trouble" and "boy" are equally acceptable. But a distinction must be made between the two in a later stage of sentence construction when the determiners—"a" or "some," for example—are to be chosen. The application of rules in sequence will be illustrated more fully below.

A second problem it solves is the theoretical one of what the bases for the classification of words and phrases should be. Generative grammar is an attempt to provide rules not for setting up classes but rather for generating sentences. Thus the problem of deciding whether verbs are in the same class because of their common meaning or their common form is not relevant. The key question is: Is it possible to generate sentences acceptable to native speakers by putting these forms in this class?

A third improvement which generative grammar offers is a motivation for the kind of diagramming which we are familiar with in both traditional and structural grammar. A sentence diagram or "tree" can be set up on the basis of the ordered application of rules for its production. For example, the sentence diagrammed by immediate constituent analysis above might at a late stage in its derivation have the following tree:

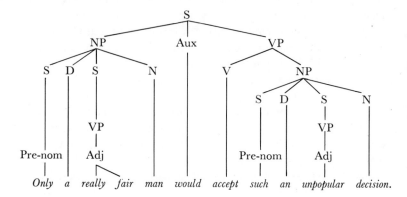

This diagram shows the application of a set of phrase-structure rules like these:

1. Rewrite S (Sentence) as NP – Aux – VP (Noun Phrase — Auxiliary — Verb Phrase).
2. Rewrite NP as D – N – S – S (Determiner — Noun — Sentence — Sentence).
3. Rewrite VP as V – NP (Verb — Noun Phrase).
4. Rewrite VP as Adj (Adjective).

It involves some transformations such as the following:

5. When the S following D – N consists of NP – Adj, rewrite D – N – S as D – Adj – N; for example, the string "The man—the man is really fair— . . ." must be rewritten "The really fair man . . ."

(*Only* and *such* are shown as derived from sentences such as "and no other man would accept such an unpopular decision" and "as this decision is unpopular." They would be derived from the S within an NP, and they would involve a familiar transformation: the deletion of repeated material. These words have been little studied, however, and it is not clear at present how they may be best accounted for.)

Some less obvious advantages of a transformational-generative approach are the economy which results from being able to describe complex sentences in terms of transformations of simple sentences, and the clarity which comes from being able to explain ambiguous constructions in terms of different structural trees.

The principal advantage of a generative approach to grammar, however, rests on the superior ability of this kind of grammar to explain the structure of sentences. As the grammar which follows will show, a generative grammar explains how a semantic structure, a proposition or a series of them, receives linguistic expression. It shows by means of an ordered series of rewriting rules how an underlying structure consisting of simple subject-predicate relations is developed into phrases and ultimately receives a phonological form. This focus on the hierarchial nature of the structure of sentences and of the underlying similarity of sentences, despite surface differences, is what distinguishes a generative approach to grammar from the approaches mentioned thus far. These ideas will be developed further in the discussion which follows.

Topics for Investigation

1. Look up the word "grammar" in an etymological dictionary. To what extent do the current connotations of the word reflect its earlier associations with subjects other than rule formation?

2. Judgments of grammaticality range from the indisputably grammatical to the indisputably ungrammatical. Constructions of doubtful grammaticality are usually "relatively" grammatical; that is, given the right context, they are grammatical. Comment on the grammaticality of these sentences:

> a. I want out.
> b. No, Mommy, I want my big, big doll.
> c. It ain't me you're lookin' for, Babe.
> d. My brother in Mexico, he is much big.
> e. The rain, which everyone including even the United States Weather Bureau had predicted would come before all the crops were harvested, fell.
> f. The man whose car which Ed bought wasn't running well left town.

3. What aspects of school grammar do adults remember best? Conduct a survey among your acquaintances to determine what they remember. It will probably be best to use questions which require them to phrase rules and find terms. What do your findings show about the probable contribution of school grammar training to an adult's understanding of and skill in using language?

4. What grammatical terms are in common use in ordinary English? For one week, keep track of the grammatical terms that occur in your general listening and reading. What do your findings suggest about the need for including grammar among the "general education" subjects in the schools?

5. Using the definitions of the parts of speech given earlier in this chapter, classify all the words in the first sentence on page 12. What difficulties do you find?

6. Make an analysis of several compositions written by children in grades 3–7. What characteristics mark their style as immature? A good approach might be to rewrite several compositions in your own style and see what changes you have to make.

7. As a kind of corrective overstatement, grammar books sometimes say: "You cannot tell what part of speech a word belongs to unless you see the word in a sentence." To what extent is this true? You can find part of the answer by consulting a dictionary which labels words according to their part of speech.

Suggestions for Further Reading

Some grammars which are in the school tradition include *English in Action*, Courses 1–4, and *Grammar in Action*, by J. C. Tressler and D. C. Christ (Boston: D. C. Heath & Company, 1960 and 1962), and *English Grammar and Composition*, by J. E. Warriner (New York: Harcourt, Brace & World, Inc., 1965). *Discovering Your Language*, by Neil Postman (New York: Holt, Rinehart & Winston, Inc., 1963) and *Exploring Your Language*, by Postman and H. Damon (New York: Holt, Rinehart & Winston, Inc., 1966) use a structural approach. This approach is also followed in David A. Conlin and Nell C. Thompson, *Our Language Today* (New York: American Book Company, 1967). A generative approach is used in the *Roberts English Series*, by Paul Roberts (New York: Harcourt, Brace, & World, Inc., 1966), in *Elementary School English*, by Anne Kirby (Palo Alto: Addison-Wesley Publishing Company, 1967), and in *Grammar I* and *Grammar II*, by Roderick A. Jacobs and Peter S. Rosenbaum (Boston: Ginn and Company, 1967).

Some widely known traditional grammars of English include G. O. Curme, *Syntax* (Boston: D. C. Heath & Company, 1931) and Otto Jespersen, *Essentials of English Grammar* (London: George Allen & Unwin Ltd., 1933). The best known structural grammars of English include Charles C. Fries, *The Structure of English* (New York: Harcourt, Brace & World, Inc., 1952) and W. Nelson Francis, *The Structure of American English* (New York: The Ronald Press Company, 1958). The theory of transformational-generative grammar is discussed more fully in Noam Chomsky, *Aspects of the Theory of Syntax* (Cambridge: The M.I.T. Press, 1965).

For a fuller survey of the development of grammatical theory, the reader may wish to consult Francis P. Dinneen, S. J., *An Introduction to General Linguistics* (New York: Holt, Rinehart & Winston, Inc., 1967).

The Sentence

Most grammars begin with a definition of the word "sentence." This is a reflection of the general recognition of these important facts: we recognize that our utterances are made up of recurring patterns—that is, that an extended utterance does not ordinarily form a single continuous structure but rather breaks into smaller units which are repetitions of patterns already used. Our traditional marks of punctuation show that we recognize recurring grammatical patterns in written English. Furthermore, grammarians generally accept the fact that while an extended utterance such as an essay or an address may have some kind of internal connectedness throughout (a structure of assumptions leading to a conclusion, of cause and effect, of cumulative detail, or the like), this overall structure is not of the same sort as the smaller recurring structures: it is a logical or esthetic structure, not a grammatical one. The term "sentence" is usually applied to the largest recurring grammatical patterns: we say that we are beginning a new sentence when the words we are about to use are not combined grammatically with the preceding ones, but begin a new grammatical structure of their own. Grammarians have usually taken as their main task the description of the internal structure of sentences. They have tried to discover and state in general terms the common grammatical patterns which underlie the sentences we make up.

Subject and Predicate

We are familiar with two statements which attempt to do this: "A sentence is a group of words which express a complete thought" and "A sentence is a group of words which contains both a subject and a predicate." We should consider what these definitions mean and whether they actually do what they set out to do. Consider the following groups of words:

1. The dog disappeared.
2. The dog put.
3. The dog put the bone.

23

4. The dog put the bone in the hole.

5. Dog the bone the hole the in put.

If we were asked to judge the completeness of these constructions, we would almost certainly call strings 1 and 4 complete and strings 2 and 3 incomplete. "Completeness" does not seem to apply to string 5. The strings we would call "complete" we would also consider sentences. If these strings are representative, then what we mean by "completeness" is something like "having all grammatical expectations fulfilled." The word "put" requires a noun phrase completer; it requires, in addition, a place phrase. "Put" is like the rest of the word and phrase stock of English: it requires a specific degree of expansion. No speaker of English would consider punctuating as a sentence strings like "the," "over the," "has been being," "lot," and so on. We do not consider a word or a group of words to constitute a sentence unless it is "completed"—supplied with the full grammatical context which it presupposes. It is no doubt this phenomenon which has led grammarians to define the sentence as a "complete" group of words. In spoken English the same rules of grammatical completeness seem to apply. In addition, we signal by our intonation whether a given string of words is complete or not. The same string of words may be made to sound interrupted or complete depending on our intonation. Thus the definition "a group of words expressing a complete thought" does seem to state a necessary (though perhaps not sufficient) condition for our classifying a group of words as a sentence. (It goes without saying that the word "thought" in this definition must mean "grammatical construction" rather than "idea," "concept," or the like. Presumably thoughts do not have clearly defined beginnings and ends, but phrases do.)

It is clear that some words and word groups cannot occur by themselves, but must have various kinds of completers. We would not consider a group of words a sentence unless it was grammatically complete. But this definition is not sufficient to distinguish a word group like "in the house" or "the old man" from a more clearly sentence-like group such as "Time flies" or "Haste makes waste." Given a word group such as "in the house" in isolation, it is unlikely that any of us would punctuate it as a sentence. But if it occurred in a conversation, perhaps in answer to such a question as "Where did you leave the keys?" we would not hesitate to punctuate it in that way. This fact raises some very important questions. One of them is this: does our punctuation, especially in written conversation, reflect our awareness of the surface structure of phrases only, or does it reflect an awareness of something underlying that structure? For example, do we intuitively supply "I left the keys . . ." when we accept "In the house" as punctuatable as a sentence? If we answer this question in the affirmative, it implies that our notion of the sentence (and thus our rules for punctuating sentences) involves more than mere phrase completeness. It may involve the implied presence of larger structures.

It is these larger structures which grammarians are attempting to characterize when they say that sentences must contain a subject and a predicate. They are saying, in effect, that phrases like "a man" or "sells cars" cannot constitute sentences—except in situations where the missing predicate or subject is implied by the context. Grammars which use the terms "subject" and "predicate" do not always define them unambiguously. The subject of a sentence is often said to be the topic or agent (that is, doer) of the sentence, while the predicate is said to be the assertion or event to which the topic or agent is related. Grammars also often give the rule that the subject noun must agree with the predicate verb in person and number. (That is, only third person singular nouns and pronouns take verbs with the suffix -*s*.) But this rule does not seem to apply in sentences such as "It was they," where "they" is clearly the topic but the verb agrees with "It." We need to examine more closely what these traditional definitions mean.

A few examples will show that the apparent topic of the sentence is not always the word with which the main verb agrees:

6. The houses were built by Ed, not Frank.
7. What John likes is hamburgers.
8. It was my brothers that built the house.

In each case, the word on which the rest of the assertion focuses is not the word the verb agrees with. On the other hand, the verb agrees with whatever construction precedes it—a plural noun, a noun clause, or a pronoun. It is clear that we will not always identify the same entities as the subject and predicate if we try to apply both the rules "the subject is the topic of a sentence" and "the subject is the word with which the predicate verb agrees." Grammarians who use both these rules must mean something more than is immediately apparent.

Our discussion of the definition "a sentence is a group of words expressing a complete thought" showed that we regard as sentences any completed phrase (whether it consists of one or many words) so long as sufficient information is present in the larger context. "In the house" will hardly do to start a conversation, but once the question "Where did you leave the keys?" has been asked, then "In the house" is acceptable. What "In the house" lacks is "I left the keys . . .," and this is supplied from the context. What we can seem to see here is two levels of structure: a surface structure, illustrated by "In the house," and a deeper structure, illustrated by "I left the keys in the house." Similarly with sentences 6–8. While the surface structure of these sentences places the subject in such a position that it no longer agrees with the verb, we can readily convert them to structures in which the opposite is true:

9. Ed, not Frank, built the houses.
10. Hamburgers are what John likes.
11. My brothers built the house.

It looks as though our traditional definitions are compatible if we define their terms more fully. Thus we can speak of a surface subject and a deep, or underlying, subject. We can speak of a phrase as "complete" despite the absence of a subject or predicate or both if it is a surface structure whose deep structure (containing the missing subject or predicate) is clear from the context. It is the surface subject which agrees with the predicate verb. It is the deep subject which is the topic or agent of the sentence.

Even with this additional specification, however, the terms "subject" and "predicate" are not satisfactorily defined. "Topic" is not a self-explanatory word; "agent" is more clear—but many sentences do not have an agent. For example, the subject in a sentence like "Ed resembles John" is presumably "Ed"—but it is not an agent. The terms "subject" and "predicate" are names for a complex grammatical relationship which can be rephrased in a number of ways: as undergoer ("The stick broke"), possessor ("John owns property"), receiver ("John accepted the gift"), logical antecedent ("Full employment implies inflation"), logical consequent ("Our conclusion follows from these assumptions"), and many more. As terms for grammatical functions, then "subject" and "predicate" cover a wide range of meanings. If we expect to use them as exact terms in making up specific grammatical rules, where it is essential to have grammatical categories clearly defined, we will have difficulty. Despite the fact that with additional definition, the terms "subject" and "predicate" can be made more exact, they may not be the best words with which to begin the description of English sentences.

It might be well to go back to the beginning and ask the question, What leads us to think that English sentences divide into two parts? Why should we go along with traditional grammarians at all when they set up two essential parts for the deep, or basic sentence? Part of the answer has been implied in our discussion above: the minimal sentence of English which is not dependent on grammatical context to be meaningful contains at least two parts. (We are for the moment excluding greetings and exclamations.) Without depending on the context to fill in any missing grammatical parts we can say "Joe died" or "Speed kills." This is not true of "Joe" or "died" or "speed" or "kills." Thus it appears that the minimal sentence of English contains at least two parts. To argue that it contains no more than two parts would be somewhat more complicated. It would rest on evidence that a grammar of English contains at least one rule that applies to every sentence of English and that requires the use of just two and no more parts. Furthermore, no part of the sentence can be left over—not included in either part. If we assume that grammatical rules may be process rules, then we can find rules that may do what we need here. Process rules are transformational rules; they are rules that derive one construction from another. There are transformational rules that require the identification of sentence parts very much like what are traditionally called the subject and the predicate. For example, given a sentence like "John sold the car," we can form the question "Who sold the car?" Even if "John" were replaced by "The little old man who lives up the street," the question would be the same. "John" and "the little old man who lives up the street" are the same kind of construction because they are both replaceable by "who." Similarly we can form the question "What did John do?" in which "sold the car" is replaced by "did do." We would use the same pro-verb (i.e., verb substitute) form even if instead of "sold the car" we had said "paid a visit to his aging grandmother last Tuesday at nine." Thus we identify the subject by substitution in questions like "Who (or what) – predicate," and the predicate in questions like "What did – subject – do?" There is another and even more convincing transformation which requires identifying a subject-like and a predicate-like part of a sentence. This is what some grammarians call the cleft-sentence transformation. In this transformation, a sentence like "The stick broke in two" becomes "What broke in two was the stick" or "What the stick did was break in two." The cleft sentence resembles the question in the way in which it uses wh-words and the pro-verb "do." It also isolates the subject and the predicate by placing them after the verb "be" as in the example we have considered. It is clear, then, that we do need to identify a subject-like and a predicate-like unit in the basic grammar of English. We will return later to the question of the number of basic parts.

Our definition of subject is now considerably more exact: it is the first unit replaceable by "who" or "what" in sentences like "John sold the car" or "The stick broke in two." ("Who sold the car?" "What broke in two?"). The predicate is similarly better defined, because we can now see that it is the kind of construction which is replaceable by the words "what—(do)—do." ("What did John do?" "What did the stick do?"). It is clear, however, that the terms "subject" and "predicate" are coming to stand for two sets of concepts quite different from those we began with. We have moved away from the use of the terms as names of grammatical *functions*, that is, names for relations that can hold between parts of sentences, such as agent-action, toward their use as names of grammatical categories. Most modern grammarians agree that these uses are quite distinct and that a different set of terms is required for the grammatical categories. These new terms are suggested by the internal structure of what we have been calling the subject and the predicate.

It may be well to emphasize the point that was made in the preceding chapter that category and function are not the same thing. A grammatical category is a class of units—words or longer constructions—which are usable in the same way in the structure of sentences. Words such as "small," "absurd," "ominous," "feeble," and "wild" belong to the same category because they occur in the same positions in grammatical structures—they can occur after "be" as in "the dog is small, feeble, absurd, etc." They can be modified by "more," "somewhat," "rather," and the like. Their functions are varied, however. In a particular sentence they might be modifiers of nouns; in another they might be subjects or objects, as they are in a sentence like "The wild despise the feeble." Most typically, they form part of predicates following "be" or another linking word. Thus they belong to the category *adjectives*, and they are so listed in all dictionaries, but they have a variety of functions depending on the sentences in which they are used.

The terms "subject" and "predicate" are basically names for functions. The terms which are replaceable by "who/what" belong to a category, as do those replaceable by "do." The "who/what" words and phrases include "John," "the car," "the stick," "the little old man," "his aging grandmother," and the like. The "do" words and phrases include "sold the car," "broke in two," "visited his aging grandmother last Tuesday at nine," and the like. Neither category corresponds exactly to any part of speech we are familiar with, yet it is clear that because the members of each are treated alike in certain transformations these two categories must form part of a grammar of English. They are typically symbolized as NP (Noun Phrase) and VP (Verb Phrase) respectively. The reason for the use of these terms is obvious: an NP is a phrase whose head-word is a noun; a VP is a phrase whose head-word is a verb. A head-word is a word which determines the features which other words in the phrase may have. If for example we choose "patience" as the head-word of a NP we will not choose the articles "a" or "some." We will not choose the relative word "who" or the adjective "fat." Similarly, if we choose "put" as the head-word of a VP, we must choose an object and place phrase. We can now say that in the deep grammar of the English sentence there will be the categories NP and VP. The sequence NP – VP defines the terms "subject" and "predicate" in the sense that the deep grammar NP will be interpreted as the subject of the predicate represented by the VP. The reverse is not true, that is, the terms "subject" and "predicate" do not define the NP and VP.

Let us now return to another structural feature of sentences which undergo the question transformation and the cleft-sentence transformation. Notice that when we convert "John sold the car" to "What did John do?" we replaced what we have called the VP. But there is one feature of this sentence which is not replaced and which does not form part of the NP: this is the feature Past. "Sold" is the result of adding past tense to "sell." "Did" is the result of adding past tense to "do." It is clear that when "sold the car" is transformed to "what-did-do," the element Past remains. We can say more accurately that the string "Past – sell – the – car" becomes "what – Past – do – do." The element Past is not replaced either in the transformations isolating the NP or in those isolating the VP. It is for this reason that some modern grammarians regard it as a separate element not forming part of either of the basic phrases. The element Past is only one of several alternatives that could be chosen. These include Non-past, "have," "be," or one of the Modal Auxiliaries such as "will," "may," "can," and the like. These elements can all be symbolized as Aux. The formula for the sentence in the deep structure of English must then be something like

$$S \longrightarrow NP - Aux - VP$$

(There is by no means general agreement about placing Aux outside the VP, and teachers should be aware that many school materials place Aux inside the VP thus:

$$S \longrightarrow NP - VP$$
$$VP \longrightarrow Aux - Vb$$

Or, to put it another way, the Verb Phrase consists of an Auxiliary and a verb with its completers.)

Before we begin to talk about the internal structure of the NP and VP, it may be well to summarize what we have said so far. We have pointed out that the traditional statements "a sentence is a group of words containing a complete thought," "a sentence must contain a subject and a predicate," "the subject is the topic of the sentence and the predicate is an assertion about it," and "the subject and verb must agree in number" do give valid information about the structure of English sentences. They need further clarification, however. The terms "subject" and "predicate" should probably be reserved for the names of grammatical *functions;* the grammatical *categories* are NP (Noun Phrase) and VP (Verb Phrase). In the deep grammar (but not necessarily in any particular spoken sentence) the sentence consists of an NP and a VP. This can be demonstrated by the question transformation and by the cleft-sentence transformation. Furthermore, the term Aux should be included in the deep grammar as one of the earliest rules. The deep grammar is the simple, complete grammatical structure which we can think of as underlying surface structures. Surface structures may show deletion, rearrangement, and the addition of various forms. They are related by process rules to underlying structures.

The NP

Most modern grammarians define the noun phrase as Determiner – Noun – Sentence: NP $\longrightarrow$ D – N – (S). The head-word—the word on which the form of D and S depends—is the noun. We usually define nouns as names of persons, places, and things. This definition is, of course, one presented in schoolbooks so that children will have some sort of frame or testing device for identifying nouns in particular sentences. It is not (and is probably not intended to be) a definition in the sense that it identifies a class of words with common grammatical characteristics. If we took it literally we would have great difficulty justifying the inclusion of words like "blunder," "lapse," and "grief," with the other nouns. Structural grammarians have defined nouns as those words occurring in phrases with determiners (words like "the" and "a"), having suffixation for plural number, and occurring in specified positions in sentences. The schoolbook definitions of grammatical terms will usually work pretty well when applied to schoolbook problems, but they present all sorts of difficulties when applied to, say, a page of a newspaper. Both schoolbook and structural definitions, however, share the common difficulty that they provide a means of classifying words in a surface structure, but they are not adequate to deal with complex sentences in which several layers or steps of sentence generation need to be identified. For example the word "building" in a phrase such as "the building of houses" does not seem to be the name of a person, place or thing. It does not permit suffixation for plural or possession. It has a determiner, "the," but (except, perhaps, for "some") that is the only determiner it can have. "A," "each," "every," etc. will not work. Furthermore, it is clear that "building" here is verb-like in a way that it is not in "a new wooden building." It seems clear then that "the building of houses" can best be understood as a sentence, filling a position that would normally be occupied by a noun. Neither the whole phrase nor the word "building" is inherently a noun in the way that such words as "grief," "foliage," "heir," and the like are nouns.

A definition of the word "noun," then, in terms of semantic features all nouns are thought to share (e.g., person, place, or thing) or of structural features, such as suffixation and function words, does not seem adequate. On the other hand, there is no doubt that the potential uses in English sentences of such words as "grief," "foliage," and "heir" are different from those of "small," "heavy," and "thick," or "retain," "disturb," and "conform." That is, if dictionary entries are to be a guide to the use of words—if they are to show the situations, semantic or grammatical, in which words may be used—they will need to show that "grief," "foliage," and "heir" belong to a special class which does not include "retain," "small," etc. But knowing which words are nouns does not seem to be a matter of knowing one or more touchstones for identifying them; rather it means knowing that in a given wide range of constructions we can use the words we usually call nouns but not words we usually call verbs, adverbs, etc. That is, nouns are a kind of prime—they make up a class whose existence we presuppose but which we cannot specify exactly. Thus the school definition, "names of persons, places, and things" is not really a bad point of departure if it is taken to mean "nouns are words you can use in the way you use the names of persons, places, and things."

The Determiner

The NP contains two structures in addition to the noun itself. These are the determiner, usually abbreviated D, and a sentence from which are derived the various noun modifiers such as adjectives and participles as well as noun clauses. The determiner (each NP includes only one) is selected from the class of words containing "a," "the," "some," etc.; or it is included in a pronoun. In most respects the subclass of the determiner is automatically selected by the noun. For example, nouns are subclassified into count nouns ("dog," "book," "table") and noncount nouns ("patience," "milk," "steel"). Count nouns automatically take "a" or another unit-specifying word such as "one" or "each" if they are singular. They take "some" or another plural-specifying word such as "two," "three," "several," "many," "all," or the like if they are plural. The noncount (or mass) nouns take either "$\emptyset$" as their determiner (that is, the determiner is viewed as occurring only in the deep structure but deleted in the surface structure) or they take such words as "much," "little," and "some." Nouns may also be proper ("Ed," "France," "mankind"). These nouns take no determiner in the surface structure, but, like the noncount nouns, may be replaced by pronouns with implicit determiners.

Determiners are traditionally called definite or indefinite. The definite determiners are "the" and the demonstratives "this," "that," "these," and "those." Indefinite determiners include "a," "some," "many," and the like. We choose definite and indefinite determiners according to the larger grammatical context rather than according to the noun subclass. For example, in the sentence series "A man and a woman were walking down the street. The man was carrying a bag," we could not replace the second "the" with "a" unless we wished to refer to a man other than the one just mentioned.

The determiners "a," "some (any)," and "the"—all of which are selected according to grammatical features of the noun they modify—are usually called articles. "This," "that," "these," and "those," the so-called demonstratives, give information about proximity as well as definiteness and number. The other determiners give additional sorts of information: "Many" and "few," which seem best classified as indefinite, count determiners, give information about quantity. "Each," "every," and "all" signal inclusiveness, by contrast to "several," "many," and "much." The determiners thus constitute a small, closed class from which we choose items partly according to the noun we have chosen and partly according to larger features of the grammatical and semantic context.

Sentences in NP's

Our grammatical tradition includes under the heading "adjectives" all those words (and phrases) which modify nouns. But it is clear that not all noun modifiers are alike. A noun can be modified by a noun ("a distribution problem"), a verb ("our rapidly disappearing resources"), or by what is in all dictionaries called an adjective ("a good man"). The schoolbook suggestion that all noun modifiers constitute an identifiable group is a good one; it suffers, however, from a confusion of the relation "modification" with the structural fact "forming part of the NP." But modern grammarians seem generally agreed that there is indeed something important in common among the various noun modifiers. This is the fact that noun modifiers like those illustrated above seem to be the result of the same transformation—the transformation of a sentence attached to a noun into a phrase in which the parts identical to those already stated are deleted. For example in the sequence "The stream was running rapidly. The stream soon changed its course" we can delete "the stream was" and obtain "The stream running rapidly soon changed its course." We can then rearrange the parts of this string to obtain "The rapidly running stream . . ." In just the same way we can get "The feeble man. . ." from "The man was feeble . . ." or "The beaten pup . . ." from "The pup was beaten . . ." (Notice that in the last two examples the rearrangement by which the modifier is placed before the noun is required in most instances.) The relative clause and its reductions and reorderings will be discussed in the next chapter.

The S which forms part of the NP can take a different from. Compare the sentence "I accepted the solution that Betty proposed" and "I accepted the fact that Betty proposed." The first means "Betty proposed a solution and I accepted it" while the second has the possible reading "Betty proposed and I accepted that fact." In the second sentence the string "that Betty proposed" is not a modifier of the preceding noun but a restatement of it—the fact is that Betty proposed. This S is traditionally called a noun clause. It occurs as a specific restatement for such words as "idea," "news," "discovery," and the like and it is thus analogous to an "appositive," or repetition by means of a synonym. It also occurs with the pronoun "it." Notice the similarity between these sentences: "The news that we were going to invade Colombia upset me" and "It upset me that we were going to invade Colombia." The first has the alternative form "The news upset me that we were going to invade Colombia" while the second can read "That we were going to invade Colombia upset me." It appears that "it" must be deleted when the noun clause immediately follows it. Thus the NP may contain either an adjective-like or appositive-like sentence, which may be reduced by deletion of repeated materials and which may occur in various positions in the NP or the whole sentence.

The NP can thus be seen to consist of a noun, a determiner, and one or more optional sentences. It can be symbolized as $D - N - (S)$. It should be emphasized that this is a rule for the NP in the deep structure. In the surface structure, the D or N may be deleted, and the S, which is always optional, may be reduced to a single word or phrase.

Pronouns

Pronouns are traditionally said to be substitutes for nouns. The concept of substitution is not a simple one: almost any word is in some sense a substitute for some other word. For example, a general word substitutes for a more specific one, as in "John has a new convertible. The car gives him a lot of pleasure." Some words, such as "thing," "object," "being," and "person," are substitutable for very large numbers of other words. Words such as "the following," "the above," and "the aforementioned," are substitutes for larger or smaller stretches of language. But there is a class of words which substitute in a more specific way. This class includes such words as "he," "they," and "it." These words are representations of grammatical features of preceding (or, rarely, following) NP's. It is clear that in the sequence "A man got out of the car. The man had a box of tools," the phrase "The man" could be replaced by "He." "He" signals the information "definite," "count," "singular," "animate," "male." "Man," of course, means "human." By contrast to "boy," it means "old." "He" does not necessarily mean "human" or "old"; it provides only the minimum information needed to assure that its reference is understood: it makes it clear, as does the phrase "the man," that the immediately preceding (i.e., definite), singular, count, animate, male noun is being referred to. "They," "she," and "it" also give information about definiteness, number, and sex. The pronouns "you," "I," and "we" are not substitutes in the sense that a specific phrase such as "the person speaking" or "the person spoken to" can be substituted for them. Despite the fact that a reasonable definition of "I" would be "the person speaking," we could not use any other phrase for "I" without being misunderstood. Even the use of one's own name would probably get a response like "Oh, does someone else have the same name as yours?" Thus "I," "we," and "you" are not in the ordinary sense substitutes. But they are like "he," "they," etc. in many important respects: they signal definiteness and number; they may be followed by nouns in so-called appositive constructions ("I, Ed Peterson, . . ."); they have an alternative form with "-self" which occurs just where it would be expected with the other pronouns; and like the others they have special forms which appear in the surface structure of sentences showing whether they are used as subjects, objectives, or possessives. Thus the pronouns seem to be one of the forms which the NP can take in English grammar. They replace the NP in constructions involving the repetition of the same noun or involving the mention of the person speaking or spoken to.

The pronouns discussed so far are usually called personal pronouns. Our tradition also classifies as pronouns a number of other words such as "one," "each," "both," "everything," "this," "which," and "that." These words divide into groups according to the rules which seem to explain their derivation best. For example, there is an obvious analogy between the sentences "I haven't seen the movie but John has seen it" and "I haven't seen a movie but John has seen one." "It" and "one" appear to be alike except for the fact that "It" replaces a NP containing a definite determiner while "one" replaces an indefinite one. "One" has another important use: it serves as a noun replacive in sentences in which the noun is identical to a preceding one but the noun modifiers are different as in "He got the/a good melon and I got the/a bad one." Notice that when it replaces only the noun it may occur in either a definite or indefinite NP. Another set of so-called pronouns seems to be more correctly described as determiners used as substitutes for NP's in which the remainder of the phrase has been deleted. The demonstratives can be used in this way: "I don't approve of that suggestion but I do like this." The process of deleting a repeated word or phrase (called identity deletion) is widely used in English grammar and seems to be the obvious explanation of phrases of this type. This process is also used in constructions involving words such as "both," "many," "few," etc. These words occur in phrases like "both of the boys," or "many of the books." When the NP in the "of"-phrase is repeated, it may be deleted, as in "Both of the boys like music and both play instruments." Notice that the word "of" is deleted along with the NP which follows it.

The words "everything," "something," "nobody," etc. also constitute a class commonly called "pronouns." Since they are not substitutes in the sense in which we have been using the word, but instead seem to be set phrases of very wide semantic generality, they do not require special discussion.

The other words commonly called "pronouns" are the relative and interrogative words, such as "who," "which," and "what." These words are substitutes—that is, they incorporate certain grammatical features which identify them as replacements for phrases which are specified in the deep structure of sentences, and which are repetitions of previously mentioned phrases. They replace complete $D - N - S$ structures, as we can see in examples like "The friendly people of Plumcreek *who* welcome you to their resorts . . ." where "who" seems to replace the entire preceding phrase. It is clearly definite as well as human. It is not marked for number. The use of "who" instead of "whom" is determined by the word's use in its own clause. These words will also be discussed further in the next chapter.

The following diagram summarizes what we have said about the NP thus far. The square brackets contain terms for grammatical features. The arrows reading across from the N to the D column indicate that these noun features imply corresponding features in the determiners. The arrows leading from N to the NP's under S show the features of the N which determine the form of a pronoun or relative word used to replace an identical N in S.

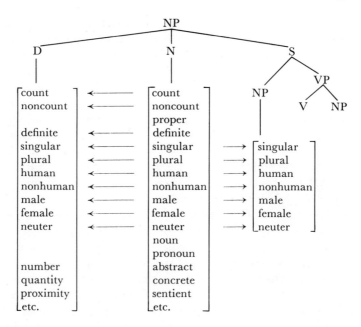

Note that proper nouns are definite only because they are replaced by personal pronouns; they do not ordinarily take "the." The features "human" and "nonhuman" are required within the noun phrase only to allow the correct selection of "who" or "which." The features "male," "female," and "neuter" are also required to assure the correct use of "he," "she," and "it." Notice that some determiner features are not automatically selected according to the noun subclassification. Notice also that some noun features do not affect the choice of a determiner. These features are instead related to the larger grammatical and situational contexts. The processes the chart represents, the formation of the determiner according to the features of the noun and the formation of the pronoun or wh-word according to the features of the whole NP, are now usually referred to as transformations.

The Verb Phrase

In our discussion above, we called the VP a verb-headed construction. This remark will have to be qualified somewhat, but it is a good place to begin. It is part of the equipment of every speaker of English to know that words like "disappear," "retain," "destroy," "compose" are much more similar to each other in the way they are used in sentences than they are to "cabinet," "truth," and "drama," or to "well," "away," and "very," or to "happy," "sweet," and "good." We are thus dealing with a class which we recognize intuitively in the same way that we recognize the class "nouns." Again, however, it is very difficult to identify any touchstones or sure clues to the identity of verbs. Instead, we are aware of a whole range of constructions in which these words can occur but in which the others are not permitted. We know that we can say "John disappeared," "John will disappear," or "Disappear!" We know that if we ask the question "What did John do?" the answer will be "(He) disappeared." Thus dictionaries which label some words "verb" give us valuable information about how those words can be used. But the VP is not necessarily just a verb with modifiers. Some VP's contain NP's, like "constructed diagrams" or "sold people cars." Others contain obligatory phrases of other kinds: "put the book on the table" or "informed me of his plans" or "grew lazy." "Put the book," "informed me," and "grew" (in the sense "became") are not acceptable English VP's. Furthermore, there is a whole range of constructions with "be," all of which include obligatory completers. (A sentence like "God is, and all is well" uses "be" in the rather rare sense "exists.") What this means is that, as in the case of the noun, verbs must be subcategorized according to features which specify the constructions with which they co-occur. There is considerable disagreement about how these features should be represented, although the grammatical facts are clear enough. It is clear that a verb such as "build" is only going to occur in a construction in which (at some point in the derivation of the sentence) it is followed by an NP. Thus even a sentence like "John builds" permits the question "What does John build?" This can be contrasted to a sentence like "John sulks," which does not permit an analogous question. A sentence which contains "put" is going to have a place-phrase somewhere in its derivation, as well as an NP. It is also important to notice that not all verbs which are followed by NP's permit the same transformations. For example, we can say "The doctor was criticized by Bill" but not "The doctor was resembled by Bill" or "The doctor was become by Bill." Thus it is necessary to show whether a verb is transitive (i.e., has the passive transformation illustrated in the preceding sentence) or intransitive. It is also necessary to indicate whether, if it is not transitive, the NP following the verb includes or is a synonym for the subject NP or not. Thus in "John resembled a doctor" and "John became a doctor" we can see two quite different relations between "John" and "a doctor." The verb "resemble" is said to be a middle verb because it is not transitive or intransitive. "Weigh" (in the sense "be of a certain weight"), "own," and "have" (in the sense "possess") are other examples of middle verbs. They not only lack a passive transformation, but they also do not have the progressive aspect (that is, we cannot say "I am having a dollar"), and they do not occur as imperatives. "Become," "grow," "get" (in the sense "become"), and a few others are often called linking verbs. They take either adjective or NP completers. There are a number of additional verb subcategories which are related to the adverbs which can modify them. For example, verbs like "walk" and "make" both take such manner adverbs as "effortlessly," "with difficulty," and the like. But such verbs as "glisten" and "pertain" do not take such adverbs. The former are usually called action verbs. It is clear that the action subcategorization cuts across both the transitive and intransitive verbs. Other verb sub-categories which can be identified but which we will not discuss in detail include those that must have animate subjects ("understand"), those that must have animate objects ("slay"), those that must form phrases with human nouns ("describe" takes a human subject, "inform" takes a human indirect object, "marry" takes both a human subject and a human direct object), those that have sentence objects ("ask," "persuade"), and many others. In a summary of this kind we will not attempt to describe them in detail. The transformations which are discussed in the following chapter do, however, require at least the following verb subcategories:

$$V \longrightarrow \begin{bmatrix} \text{transitive } [/\_\_\text{NP (Passive)}] \\ \text{intransitive} \\ \text{middle } [/\_\_\text{NP}] \\ \text{linking } \left[/\_\_ \begin{Bmatrix} \text{Adj} \\ \text{NP} \end{Bmatrix} \right] \end{bmatrix}$$

(The structural terms included in brackets are obligatory parts of the phrases in which the various verb subcategories occur.)

The Auxiliary

In our discussion above we showed that the Auxiliary is a part of the base grammar and that it must be specified very early in the derivation of any sentence. The English auxiliary words are the modals ("will," "shall," "may," "must," "can"), "have," "be"; and their variant forms such as "would," "has," "was," etc. It is useful to speak of Tense as an Auxiliary in English. We form phrases with auxiliaries according to this pattern:

Tense	Modal	Perfect	Progressive

$$\begin{Bmatrix} \text{Present} \\ \text{Past} \end{Bmatrix} - \left(\begin{Bmatrix} \text{will} \\ \text{shall} \\ \text{may} \\ \text{must} \\ \text{can} \end{Bmatrix} \right) - \text{(have-en)} - \text{(be-ing)} - \text{Verb}$$

We observe the following rules: Only Tense (Present or Past) is obligatory. Tense is applied to the unit immediately following it. Any or all of the other auxiliary words may be chosen, but they must remain in this order. If "have" is chosen, the following item will have its "-en" (i.e., past participle) form. If "be" is chosen, the following item will end with "-ing."

As the pattern shows, Tense is limited to Present and Past. It must be emphasized that the term Tense is here being used to classify a group of related grammatical features (with their semantic correlates). It is not being used interchangeably with "time"—a much more complicated concept. We can express many time subdivisions, including the familiar past, present, and future and an amazing number of others, signaled by such words as "during," "while," "then," "later," and the like. But we are not talking about subdividing time; we are talking about the phenomenon of word-form change by which "will" becomes "would," "talk" becomes "talked," and "have" becomes "had." The base form of the verb and the base plus the suffix "-(e)s" are called the Present tense forms of the verb. The suffixed form is selected by a third person singular subject (that is, a subject which can be replaced by "he," "she," or "it"). Otherwise the simple form is used. The Past tense form is the form with the suffix "-ed" or one of its variants. These variants include partial replacement, illustrated by "drive" and "drove," complete replacement, illustrated by "go" and "went," a combination of suffixation and replacement, illustrated by "sleep" and "slept," and ∅, illustrated by "cut." The Past form does not vary according to the person of the subject.

An important reason for regarding Tense as an independent unit in the structure of the Auxiliary is the fact that Tense does not necessarily occur as an affix of a verb or one of the other auxiliary words already mentioned. Notice that the sentences "John sings well" and "Does John sing well?" contain the same basic components, an NP, a verb, a manner adverb, and the element which is represented by "-s" in the first example and by "does" in the second. It is clear that to form questions of this type in English we must separate the element Tense and place it at the beginning of the sentence, where it is attached to the dummy auxiliary "do." The same thing is true with negations, as the sentences "John sings well" and "John doesn't sing well" show. These forms will be discussed further in the next chapter.

The selection of the modals "will" and "shall" together with a main verb or an auxiliary and a main verb is often called the future tense. We may have developed this tradition from the fact that real future tenses, such as those in Latin or French, may be translated with these auxiliaries in English. But these words are used in the same way as the other modals, and there seems to be no grammatical reason for considering them a separate class. And, of course, their meaning is quite often not future at all. For example, the question, "Will you help me?" is an inquiry about willingness, not future occurrences; and "Shall we wake him?" has the meaning "Is it proper?" "Would it be right?", not "Is it going to happen?"

The form of the auxiliary is a very complex part of English grammar. Notice that the modals lack the third person singular marker "-(e)s," a feature that distinguishes them from "have" and "be." Notice also that the past form of the modals must be chosen in constructions where the present might be expected. This usually occurs in the main clauses modified by "if"-clauses as in "If he came, I would help him," but it also occurs without explicit "if"-clauses, as in the sentence preceding this one. Further complexities appear when the modals occur in certain transformations. For example, we can make up infinitive phrases headed by any verb. Such phrases may also contain either or both of the auxiliaries "have" and "be," but not the modals. We can say "for John to go," ". . . to have gone," ". . . to be going," or ". . . to have been going." But we cannot say "for John to will go." Instead of the modals we use a semantically similar set of phrases including "to be willing to," "to have to," "to be able to," "to be permitted to," "to be going to" and the like. The same set of alternates is optional in most other circumstances. Notice, however, that these alternates sometimes supply missing tense forms (for example, "He must leave now," "He had to leave yesterday"). Notice also that the use of the present and past forms of the modals is not parallel. Compare "He can sing now and he could sing yesterday" with *"He shall sing now and he should sing yesterday" and *"He may sing now and he might sing yesterday." The problem of selection of modal forms has hardly been dealt with at all in generative grammar, and the best studies are still the traditional ones mentioned at the end of this chapter.

"Have" and "be" have their own complexities. The various forms of each cause part of this problem. "Be" is the only form in English which has a form change reflecting first, second, and third persons in the present tense or singular and plural number in the past. As has been noted above, not all verbs can occur with "be-ing" as the auxiliary, a fact which causes the native speaker little difficulty but can be very difficult for a foreign learner of English. There is some evidence that the use of both "be" and "have" differs according to social class dialect. For example, in some class dialects "be" is usually unexpressed in constructions like "He (is) going home now." The omission of "have" in a sentence like "I done that five times" seems to be a matter of class dialect. For some speakers of English, however, the omission of "have" is a matter of style. Such speakers would say "I read the book five times" but write "I have read the book five times."

Adjectives

In the discussion above we have referred to adjectives several times without considering them in detail. It is necessary now to see how they fit into the base grammar of English. It has already been observed that adjectives seem to enter noun phrases in very much the same way that participles (verbs with the suffix "-ing") do. That is, we can say both "the dog is sleeping" and "the sleeping dog"; "the dog is black" and "the black dog." We apply a similar transformation to nouns: "the box is for hand-

kerchiefs"; "the handkerchief box." If we consider the structure Determiner
– Adjective – Noun to be derived in the same say that Determiner – Verb –
Noun and Determiner – Noun – Noun structures are derived we reflect the
assumption that there is an underlying simplicity in the grammar of English
—that instead of a large number of different basic structures, we have a
relatively few structural units and transformational processes by which we
produce our great variety of surface structures. While we must identify a
basic category called Adjective, we need not develop a new structural
pattern for the basic NP, since we can show that adjectives occur in the NP
in the same way as other items from the VP, including both noun and verb
forms.

Some grammarians believe that adjectives are sufficiently similar
to verbs that they can properly be called subcategories of the same basic
unit. There are some obvious relations between verbs and words traditionally called adjectives; for example, we can say either "He destroys" or "He
is destructive." The same modifiers can occur with both sentences: We
can say "He destroys (is destructive) without motivation, constantly, for the
pleasure of it" and the like. There are also some similarities between adjectives and nouns: compare "It was a monster" and "It was monstrous."
But words like "small," "feeble," "mild," and thousands of others seem not
to be derived from nouns or verbs. It is difficult to see how they can be a
subcategory of one any more than the other. Like other basic structural
units (D, NP, N, etc.) they seem to be definable only in terms of a total
grammar of which they form a part. It is worth noting that adjectives have
their own class of modifiers, words like "very," "rather," "somewhat,"
"awfully," "too," etc. They have the possibility of comparison, either with
"-er" and "-est" or "more" and "most," "less" and "least." They appear
in the VP under two circumstances: either as a completer of a small list of
linking verbs, including "become," "remain," "get," "grow," "stay," and
a few others; or following the word "be."

Adverbs

Our school grammar (unlike the better traditional grammars)
gives us little useful information about adverbs. It is clear that the words
that "modify verbs" are quite different from those that "modify adjectives
and other adverbs." The former group must include such constructions as
"with difficulty," "effortlessly," and the like. The latter includes "very,"
"rather," "somewhat," "too," "awfully," and a few others. It is clear that
there is little overlap between these groups. While we can say both "She
sings agreeably" and "She is agreeably thin," we cannot say both "She
talks energetically" and "She is energetically thin." That is, there is a set
of adverbs that can accompany action verbs but that are not permitted with

adjectives unless they have been derived from action verbs. The same thing is true of time and place phrases, though this is somewhat more complicated: we cannot say "She was tall in Spain," although we can say "She was happy in Spain." Similarly we cannot say "The chest was wooden in 1956," although we can say "The chest was green in 1956." The class of words and phrases called adverbs is thus not a single large set of items, but many subsets, some members of which are never interchangeable with the others.

The simplest of the adverbs (in one way, at least) are what we will call the qualifiers. These are words like "very," "rather," and "somewhat." They modify adjectives and certain adverbs, and they resemble the comparative words "more" and "most." An important difference is that with "more" and "most" we can usually easily identify underlying sentences as in "John is upset"—"Ed is more upset": "Ed is more upset than John." At present we can say little more than that adjectives (and adverbs derived from them) can have qualifying words like those just mentioned. Whether these can best be understood as categories of the basic structure or in some other way is not clear.

By far the most numerous of the adverbs and the words we probably think of at once as examples of members of the adverb class are the words that "tell how, when, or where." What this traditional definition means is that there is a class of words and phrases characterized by having the question-word substitutes "how," "when," and "where." These are the words said to modify verbs. It is clear, however, that the words and phrases which have the substitutes mentioned above may be quite different from each other in important ways. We should notice some of these differences.

The words and phrases which have "how" as their substitute include first of all the instrument phrases. Such phrases usually begin with the preposition "with," as in the sentence "Ed cut it down with an axe." The question "How did Ed cut it down?" is thus an alternative way of saying "What did Ed cut it down with?" But some phrases beginning with "by" and "by means of" are very closely related semantically: "He broke it by applying pressure." And the passive "by"-phrase perhaps belongs in this category: "Ed was shot by George." The "how" phrases include judgments of value. They may be expressed by single words or by prepositional phrases. Thus we can say "She sang well," "She sang with "skill," or "She sang skillfully." The latter two seem to be transformationally related to "Her singing was skillful," which will be discussed below. Another important set of "how" constructions are the ordinary manner phrases like "fast," and "slow," "awkwardly," "sleepily," "angrily," "with care," "in a cautious manner," and the like. These will also be discussed below.

The time phrases, those replaceable by "when," also subdivide in important ways. Some time phrases refer to points of time. These are usually expressed by the prepositions "on," "in," and "at." The choice of prepositions is determined by the noun that follows: we say "on Sunday in

March at 6 o'clock." Other time phrases express times relative to other
specified times. For example, phrases beginning with "after," "before,"
and "during" express relative time, as do the words "early," "late," and
"soon." Still another subclass of time phrases is the set of frequency phrases
including "never," "always," "frequently," "occasionally," and the like, as
well as "once," "twice," etc.

The place phrases have two main subgroups. The first of these are the
location phrases. These are the phrases that begin with "in," "on," and "at,"
"beside," "above," "below," "over," "under," and the like followed by a
place noun. In some instances the choice of prepositions seems to be determined by the noun: "in Spain," "on Sixth Street," "at my house." Others
are determined by the verb: we *put in* or *on*, not *at;* we *push on* a direct
object; *convey* something *to* but not *at*. The other main group of place phrases
are the direction phrases. These are the phrases that begin with "into,"
"onto," "toward," as well as most of the place prepositions already mentioned.

There would be no point in mentioning these adverb subclasses if
there were no differences in their uses in the construction of sentences.
But there are several such differences. One of the most obvious and superficial is their position relative to each other and to the other parts of the
sentence. It is obvious that place phrases must precede time phrases: we
say "Ed went there then," not *"Ed went then there." Furthermore, there
are severe restrictions on their occurrence elsewhere in the sentence. We
do not say *"In Spain he lived in 1956" although we can say "In 1956 he
lived in Spain." Similarly we can say "He left Washington unexpectedly in
1956" but probably not *"He died in 1956 unexpectedly." Some of these
restrictions are probably explainable merely as compounding order rules
analogous to those that require us to say "a little old lady" and not *"an
old little lady." But others must be explained by differences in the deeper
structure of sentences. Let us notice what some of these differences may be.
Notice that we accept these sentences:

> Students protested frequently in 1968.
> Students frequently protested in 1968.
> In 1968 students protested frequently.
> (Perhaps) Students in 1968 protested frequently.

but not these:

> *Frequently students protested in 1968.
> *Students frequently in 1968 protested.
> *Students protested in 1968 frequently.

If we identify the sentence parts in this way:

> A   B   C   D
> *Students protested frequently in 1968.*

we see that we will accept the strings:

> ABCD
> ACBD
> DABC
> ADBC

but not:

> ABDC
> ACDB
> CABD

That is, we do not accept the strings in which B and C are separated. We keep "frequently" next to "protested," although we move "in 1968" about freely. This suggests that the frequency adverb has a different—and closer— relation to the verb than does the point-of-time adverb. This difference may be represented in this way:

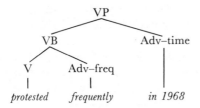

What we appear to be doing is making sure that "frequently" modifies "protested." That is, we want to say that what occurred in 1968 was that students protested frequently. We do not want to say that what occurred frequently was that students protested in 1968. (The symbol VB is introduced to represent a substructure within the VP consisting of a verb and an element more closely connected to it than other parts of the VP including certain adverbs. It is possible that the time adverb could be attached directly to S, but it is clearly different in its privileges of occurrence from such sentence-modifying adverbs as "of course," "nevertheless," and the like.)

We can see a similar distinction between the adverbs in these sentences:

> The tourists got to see bullfights in Spain.
> In Spain the tourists got to see bullfights.
> The tourists in Spain got to see bullfights.
> The tourists turned their course toward France.
> *Toward France the tourists turned their course.
> *The tourists toward France turned their course.

Notice once again that one adverb phrase is more movable than the other. In these sentences we can see that a direction phrase stays firmly attached to the verb while the "static" place phrase moves about freely. While we do not ordinarily have both a direction phrase and a static place phrase in the same sentence, we nevertheless seem to require a tree diagram like the one just used to show how these adverbs are different. The direction adverb phrase is like the frequency phrase in being attached more closely to the verb than is the static place phrase. We should not make the false inference that all static place phrases are attached to a tree diagram at some point above V however. Compare these sentences:

> Tourists can see bullfights in Spain.
> My brother lives in Spain.

We can say:

> Tourists in Spain can see bullfights.
> In Spain tourists can see bullfights.

but not:

> *My brother in Spain lives.
> *In Spain my brother lives.

Thus there are clearly some verbs, such as "live," which require adverb phrase completers. The adverbs completing such verbs must be attached so that their close relation to the verb is made clear.

Some adverbs are traditionally said to modify sentences. Constructions commonly called sentence-modifying adverbs include "afterward," "for that reason," "in that way," "undoubtedly," "of course," and the like. It has recently been suggested that at least some adverbs with an adjective base can also be understood best as sentence-modifying adverbs. Consider the sentence:

> He gave her the car unexpectedly.

This sentence, like the others we have just discussed, permits several different word orders: "unexpectedly" may come first or it may come after "He." It may not, however, separate the verb from either the indirect or direct object. This suggests that the adverb is attached to the sentence at a level above the VP. Because "unexpectedly" is derived from an adjective, a possible underlying structure for the sentence might look like this.

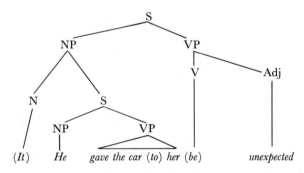

(In this and several other diagrams where Aux is represented by verb suffixation, the derivation of the auxiliary is not shown.) Some transformations which must obviously be performed include the deletion of the unneeded parts of the underlying sentence containing the adjective, and the addition of "-ly" to "unexpected" as a result of its being attached to "He gave her the car."

Whether this analysis is correct or not remains to be determined. The fact that we can readily make up what seem to be obvious transformations of the structure represented by the tree suggests that it may be correct: we can say "His giving her the car was unexpected" or "His unexpected giving of the car to her" or "It was unexpected his giving her the car" or "What was unexpected was his giving her the car." In any case, it is clear that there is a very important relation between adverbs and adjectives. While we noted above that there were no action adjectives except those derived from verbs (that is, we cannot say things like "He was tall energetically") there are some adjectives that are applicable to occurrences, and these adjectives have corresponding adverb forms. We cannot say "It was a sudden table" but we can say "It was a sudden change in the weather"; we cannot say "It was a quick pencil" but we can say "It was a quick summary." There is a clear relation between the set of words including the adjectives which modify nouns naming occurrences, the adverbs corresponding to those adjectives, and the verbs corresponding to those nouns. We can say "The weather changed suddenly," "It was summarized quickly." There is clearly a great deal of interchange among the parts of speech membership of English words. Notice these alternations:

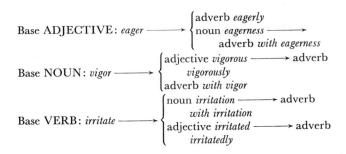

It is not clear how all of these alternations can best be included in a coherent grammar, but there seems to be little doubt that a series like "Something irritated him," "His reply was irritated," "He replied irritatedly," and "He replied with irritation" are transformations of the same grammatical material. It is perhaps most important to note that the English language provides alternatives whereby the same predication may be noun or verb headed and in which the same word may take an adjective or adverb form.

Deriving Sentences

Suppose we take a fairly simple sentence such as "John disappeared." What can we say about its structure using the grammatical framework described above? It is clear that the sentence has an NP, an Aux, and a VP. The NP contains a proper noun, and the verb is intransitive. We can represent the structure of the sentence with a diagram such as this one:

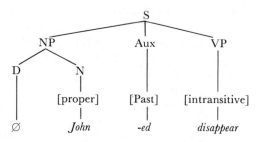

The choice of ∅ for the determiner was obligatory with a proper noun. (This is another way of saying that the article can be introduced only after the noun features are selected; there is thus an article transformation.) If we had chosen another noun, our determiner would be different. Assuming that we chose one of the articles, we would have had structures such as these:

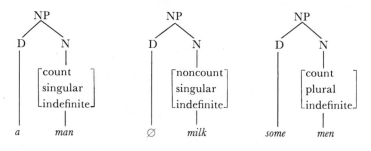

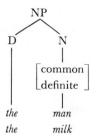

(Notice that when the noun is definite and common, the features countability and number do not affect the form of the article. The affix "-ed" is applied to the verb "disappear" by the affix transformation.)

Suppose the Auxiliary had been more complicated; suppose the sentence had read "John has disappeared." We would then have a deep structure something like:

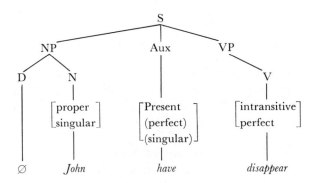

Notice that because the Auxiliary is present, it must be marked as singular or plural. The Auxiliary is singular because the preceding NP is singular. The Auxiliary is perfect because the feature "perfect" has been selected for the Verb. We must still apply the affix transformation which adds "-s" to "have" giving "has," and which adds the perfect affix to "disappear," giving "disappeared."

If we chose the feature "progressive" as well as "perfect" and "present" (that is, if we wished to say "John has been disappearing"), it is clear that the appropriate transformations would have to take place in a particular order. We would have to introduce the perfect auxiliary first. This auxiliary takes its number from the preceding noun; it specifies the suffix of the word which follows. Then we would apply the progressive transformation, inserting "be." Last of all we would add the appropriate affixes by which "have" becomes "has," "be" becomes "been" and "disappear" becomes "disappearing." If we chose a modal as well as the other auxiliaries we would find that it must be introduced first and that the number of the NP would be applicable to it, not to "have." (With modals, of course, the distinction between singular and plural is not represented by an affix.) Otherwise, we would follow the same rules in the same order.

If our sentence contained adverbs, the deep structure would have to be somewhat different. It might contain a sentence-modifying phrase such as "of course." It might also contain a time word such as "yesterday." And it might contain a direction phrase like "into the darkness." A simplified deep-structure diagram for our sentence might look like this:

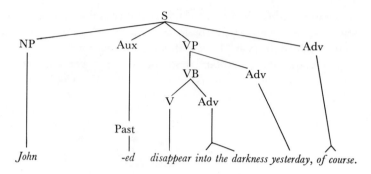

The diagram shows that "yesterday" is not merely coordinate to "into the darkness," but actually follows different rules. (It may occur in positions in the sentence where "into the darkness" is not permitted.) It also shows that "of course" follows rules different from those of either of the other adverbs.

If we had chosen a verb with different grammatical features, the deep structure of our sentence would be affected. For example, we might have chosen "drive." Our deep structure would then show something like this:

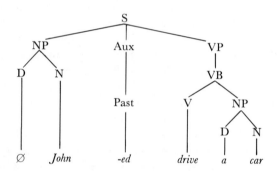

John drove a car.

A verb like "give" involves still another category in the deep structure:

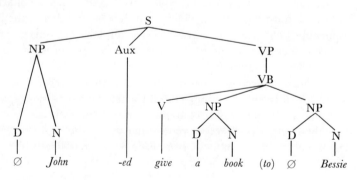

A transformation not previously mentioned which must be applied to this sentence is the introduction of "to" before the second NP. If we should rearrange the parts of this sentence (a topic we will consider in more detail in the next chapter) we would have to omit "to":

John gave Bessie a book.

The grammar we have developed thus far allows another important constituent in the deep structure of sentences: the S which follows NP or D–N. This embedded sentence will also be discussed further in the following chapter.

Topics for Investigation

1. Pay close attention to the next five or six casual conversations you participate in. What kind of sentence typically opens a conversation? What kind of sentences continue it? Do most of the sentences have both a subject and predicate? In an extended utterance by the same speaker, do you find that sentence-final pitch contours always correspond to unsubordinated subject-predicate structures?

2. Conduct an experiment to determine what structures native informants actually will accept as complete. Compile a list containing ordinary subject-predicate sentences, imperatives, abbreviated answers to questions, and word-groups you would not consider sentences. Ask your informants to identify the items on your list as sentences or nonsentences. Try to explain why your informants agreed—and disagreed—with each other. You might want to inquire about the theory on which they based their answers.

3. Examine the first ten noun phrases in any book or article. How many parts do they typically consist of? Does our formula for the NP provide for all the parts you find? What can be said about the parts we have not provided for?

4. What can you say about the "indefinite" nouns such as "somebody," "everything," "anyone"? Consider their use with determiners and other modifiers. Are they pronouns in the sense that they "replace" nouns? Do they belong to any of the noun subclasses we have mentioned?

5. (a) Are tense and time the same? Consider sentences like these: "I leave tomorrow." "I am leaving tomorrow." "Joe comes up to me and he says, 'Lay off, or I'll poke you in the nose.'"

   (b) Compare the time implications of "will" with human and nonhuman subjects.

6. "Will" and "would" can easily be demonstrated to be present and past respectively, both in time and in tense. Does this apply to the other

auxiliary sets "can-could," "may-might," and "shall-should"? What special privileges do these "past" forms seem to have with regard to their occurrence with time words like "yesterday," "tomorrow," and "now"?

7. Do the sense verbs ("look," "feel," etc.) constitute a special verb subclass? Consider the kinds of completers they can take. Do other linking verbs have exactly the same kind of completers? Can all the sense verbs be both transitive and intransitive (e.g., "He smelled the cheese" and "The cheese smelled bad")?

8. Classify these verbs as "transitive," "intransitive," or "linking."

            live   comment   span   radiate

What difficulties do you find? What does this say about the adequacy of a three-part verb subclassification?

Suggestions for Further Reading

The reader may wish to compare some other "transitional" generative grammars with the one presented above. One such grammar is Paul Roberts' *Modern Grammar* (New York: Harcourt, Brace & World, Inc., 1968), an "adult" version of the grammar which appears in the *Roberts English Series. Transformational Grammar and the Teacher of English*, by Owen Thomas (New York: Holt, Rineholt, & Winston, Inc., 1965) shows some of the ways generative grammar can be applied to lower school teaching. "Transformational Grammar" by Ralph Goodman in Norman C. Stageberg, *An Introductory English Grammar* (New York: Holt, Rinehart, & Winston, Inc., 1966) presents a way of dealing with overlapping subcategories which has much to commend it. There is brief but very usable grammar in *Generative English Handbook* by H. R. Eschliman, R. C. Jones, and T. R. Burkett (Belmont, California: Wadsworth Publishing Co., 1968).

Probably the best extended discussions of the nature of the sentence can be found in traditional grammars. One such discussion can be found in G. O. Curme, *Syntax*. The topic is also mentioned in Otto Jespersen, *Essentials of English Grammar*. The structural linguist Charles C. Fries has discussed this topic in *The Structure of English*, as has W. Nelson Francis in *The Structure of American English*.

The notion of parts of speech is discussed in Fries. On the topic of the parts of speech in first language learning, see "Three Processes in the Child's Acquisition of Syntax" by Roger Brown and Ursula Bellugi and "Imitation and Structural change in Children's Language" by Susan M. Ervin, both in Eric H. Lenneberg, *New Directions in the Study of Language* (Cambridge: The M.I.T. Press, 1964). The reader should also see Chapter VI of Roger Brown's *Words and Things* (Glencoe, Ill.: The Free Press, 1958).

An early but extremely interesting partial transformational grammar of English is Robert B. Lees, *The Grammar of English Nominalizations* (The Hague: Mouton & Co., 1960). A more recent transformational grammar is Roderick A. Jacobs and Peter S. Rosenbaum, *English Transformational Grammar* (Waltham, Mass.: Blaisdell Publishing Company, 1968).

Combining, Shortening, and Rearranging Sentences

CHAPTER In our discussion above, such phrases as "question transformation," "passive," "relative clause," and "noun clause"
have occurred. These terms are related to forms of sentences
which have not been fully specified by the rules which have
been developed so far. Every speaker of English can produce sentences
which combine with other sentences, which follow a different order than
the rules just given allow, or which replace the NP, the Adj, or the Adv
with constructions much more complicated than those we have provided
for. These sentences are produced by transformational rules which we now
want to develop more fully.

Transformations

As we have already seen, some constructions which are superficially different seem to have the same grammatical meaning: that is, they
express the same lexical content in the same grammatical relations. Some
examples include "John goes," "John's going," "For John to go," "That
John goes," as well as "who goes," the last occurring only when "John" has
already been mentioned. Furthermore, some constructions that are superficially alike are different in meaning. Compare "They made John leave"
and "They saw John leave." Notice that the first is a way of saying "They
caused-to-leave *someone*": "someone" is supplied from "John left." The second
is related to "They saw *something*"; again we supply "John left." The second
is paraphrased as "They saw John's departure," but the first does not
paraphrase as "They made John's departure." It seems clear that the
correspondence between grammatical form and grammatical function which
characterizes the output of the rules given in the preceding chapter does not
characterize all or even many of the actual sentences of English. We must

show how sentences can become NP's or modifiers; how parts of ser.tences may be deleted; how the appropriate connecting material may be added; and how the parts of sentences can undergo changes in order.

As we have shown, we need transformations to produce even the simplest sentences in English. We have seen that Tense, for example, is a separate element in English sentences; it must be attached by a transformation to the main verb or to whichever of the auxiliaries comes first. Similarly, number throughout the sentence can best be explained as being introduced through a transformation. The head noun of the subject NP seems to determine the number of its own modifiers and of its verb. We can probably best describe this phenomenon by introducing the noun with number and then adding the appropriate number to the words that agree with the noun by means of a transformation. There are other transformations which must be applied if certain optional choices are made in the basic string. For example, if we add the element "not"—or Negative—to the basic string, it, like Tense, seems to have to come before the rest of the auxiliary, somewhat like this:

$$\text{Negative} - \text{Aux} - \text{V}$$

If Negative is chosen, it is attached to the rest of the string in these possible ways:

$$\text{NP} - \text{Tense} - \begin{bmatrix} --- \\ \text{M} \\ \text{have-en} \\ \text{be-ing} \end{bmatrix} - \text{Negative} - \begin{bmatrix} --- \\ \text{(have-en)} - \text{(be-ing)} \\ \text{(be-ing)} \\ --- \end{bmatrix} - \text{V}$$

I.e., we can have NP – Tense – Negative – V; NP – Tense – M – Negative – (have-en) – (be-ing) – V, etc.

Our rules for making up yes-no questions are very similar to the rules for negation. We can add an optional element "Q" to our rules for the basic string in somewhat this way:

$$\text{Q} - \text{NP} - \text{Tense} - \text{(M)} - \text{(have-en)} - \text{(be-ing)} - \text{V}$$

If "Q" is chosen, then the order of the phrase must be changed:

$$\text{Q} - \text{NP} - \text{Tense} - \text{(M)} - \text{(have-en)} - \text{(be-ing)} - \text{V} \longrightarrow$$

$$\text{Tense} - \begin{bmatrix} --- \\ \text{M} \\ \text{have-en} \\ \text{be-ing} \end{bmatrix} - \text{NP} - \begin{bmatrix} --- \\ \text{(have-en)} - \text{(be-ing)} \\ \text{(be-ing)} \\ --- \end{bmatrix} - \text{V}$$

That is, to make up a yes-no question, NP is placed after Tense and the first auxiliary word. Notice that the process in each case is very similar: an element from another part of the sentence is placed after Tense and the first auxiliary word. Notice also this important similarity: if no auxiliary word is chosen, the Tense affix is attached to a dummy Auxiliary "do." Thus we have series like:

John can go.	John can not go.	Can John go?
John writes.	John does not write.	Does John write?

If we wish to form a negative yes-no question, such as "Doesn't John write?" we seem to follow these rules:

1. Develop the Auxiliary.
2. Move Negative to the position following Tense and the first auxiliary word, if there is one. (Negation takes the form "not" or "n't.")
3. Move NP to the position following the phrase formed from the first Auxiliary element and Negative.
4. Introduce "do" if no Aux occurs between Tense and the NP.

There are several reasons for proposing this order. First of all, it is not possible to insert Negative between auxiliary words unless these have been developed; thus Auxiliary development must precede the positioning of the negative word. Secondly, the negative word seems to form a phrase with the preceding auxiliary word, as our habitual use of such contractions as "couldn't," "hasn't," and "isn't," and "doesn't" shows. Thus we want to say that NP is placed after the first element of the Auxiliary, whether it is negative or not. Thirdly, "do" introduction must follow the other transformations because it occurs only when some element separates Tense from V.

We are, of course, describing the ordinary negative yes-no question. We should mention that there is a stylistic variation which allows the placement of the NP before Negative. This gives slightly archaic and bookish sentences such as "Has he not gone?" We should also mention that when an adverb of frequency is part of the VP, we can say either "I haven't ever seen him" or "I have never seen him." Thus there seems to be the option of attaching Negative either to the first auxiliary element or to a following "ever."

Our discussion thus far has shown that we can introduce elements such as Negative or Q (Question) into ordinary NP – Aux – VP structures. The introduction of these elements leads to such processes as reordering, affix variation, or marker introduction which signal to our listeners the new semantic content of our sentences. The processes of addition, rearrangement, and deletion are the means by which we obtain the remarkable sentence variety which English is capable of and by which we obtain the focus, economy, and logical progression which characterize good writing. We want to consider some of these alternative sentence shapes in detail.

Postnominal Modifiers

The formula for the deep structure of the Noun Phrase given above was this: $D - N - S$. The formula reflects the fact that English Noun Phrases commonly contain structures which can best be understood as derived from sentences. A sentence sequence such as "A merchant was preparing to go out of business. He was cutting prices" can be rephrased as "A merchant who was cutting prices was preparing to go out of business," or "A price-cutting merchant was preparing to go out of business." The grammatical relations between the parts of these sentences are the same; if there are differences in interpretation, they involve emphasis and style. These seem to be structures of the kind that can be understood best as coming from the same deep structure. The differences among them are the result of transformational processes applicable to all sentences with that deep structure. Its crucial features are these:

$$
\begin{array}{c}
\text{NP} \\
D - N_1 - S \\
Y - \text{NP} - Z \\
D - N_1 \\
\text{[definite]}
\end{array}
$$

What this symbolizes is the following: Any noun phrase may include a sentence which contains a repetition of the head noun. The repeated noun may occur in any position in its sentence. It must have the feature "definite." In the example given above, the noun "merchant" is repeated in the sentence "The merchant was cutting prices." The second occurrence of the word "merchant" has the definite article. If the repeated noun "merchant" had been an object instead of the subject of its sentence, we could still have reduced it to a modifying clause. For example, we could have said "The merchant was preparing to go out of business. We met him a week ago." This could become "The merchant (whom) we met a week ago was preparing to go out of business." Tree diagrams for these two structures are the following:

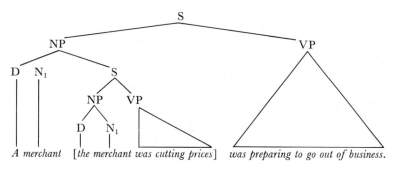

A merchant [*the merchant was cutting prices*] *was preparing to go out of business.*

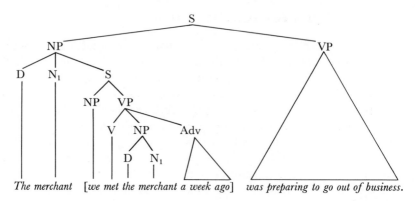

The merchant [*we met the merchant a week ago*] *was preparing to go out of business.*

We must apply these additional transformations:

> 1. Relative word introduction: the NP containing the repeated noun is replaced by "that," "which," or "who." ("Whom" is used if the repeated noun comes from the VP and is a human noun.)
>
> 2. Relative word placement: the relative word must be placed immediately after the repeated noun.

We can reduce and rearrange the relative clause in various ways: we can delete the relative word (applicable only if the repeated noun is from the VP). If the copula or auxiliary "be" is present in the embedded sentence, it may be deleted as well as the relative word. And the parts of the sentence following "be" may under certain conditions be placed between the determiner and the head noun. Notice these alternative expressions:

a man who is driving rails:	a man driving rails:	a rail-driving man
a man who is singing:	a man singing:	a singing man
a man who is from Spain:	a man from Spain:	———
a man who is tall:	———:	a tall man

What these examples show is that there are restrictions on the options we have just stated. These restrictions relate to the form of the complement of "be" in cases of relative word and "be" deletion. It is clear that some verbs with the suffix "-ing" can occur either before or after the noun they modify. If they are transitive, their objects must precede them when they occur prenominally. But prepositional phrases can only follow the nouns they modify. Adjectives, on the other hand, must precede.

The constructions we have been describing are usually called relative (or adjective) clauses. They are also usually called restrictive. The difference between restrictive and nonrestrictive clauses is illustrated by these two sequences: "Two men were crossing a footbridge. The one who was nearest the edge fell off." "A man and a woman were crossing a footbridge. The man, who was nearest the edge, fell off." The first contains a restrictive clause—the clause "who was nearest the edge" identifies the man who fell off. The second contains a nonrestrictive clause; "the man" is sufficiently identified by the context. The two clauses are distinguished in several ways: the restrictive clause can take either "who" or "that" as relative words. It is spoken without a significant speed change at its onset. While both have the alternative forms "being nearest the edge" and "nearest the edge," these alternative forms may occur preceding the head noun only when they are nonrestrictive. The second sequence can contain "Being nearest the edge, the man fell off." This is not true of the first. This difference will be discussed in greater detail below.

Noun Clauses

Certain nouns in English may be followed by sentences in which the head noun need not be repeated. Examples of such nouns are "fact," "idea," "discovery," "hypothesis," and the like. Such nouns may be followed by clauses beginning with "that." The clause beginning with "that" is somewhat like what is called an appositive in traditional grammar: it identifies the noun by providing a substitute for it. Thus we can say "The fact that today is Thursday surprises nobody." Notice that the head noun need not be repeated, and that the word "that" is not a relative word: it is only a marker identifying the following sentence as what is usually called a noun clause. The relative words "who," "which," and "whom" may not be used in place of "that." The fact that "that" clauses often occur without such a phrase as "the fact" or "the idea" has led some grammarians to regard them as an alternative form for an NP rather than as a sentence attached to a noun within an NP. There are several reasons why this may not be the best way to look at them. An important reason is the fact that noun clauses which do not occur as part of phrases with nouns do so with the pronoun "it." Thus we can say "That today is Thursday is true"; but we can also say "It is true that today is Thursday." Thus we seem to have a basic string something like this:

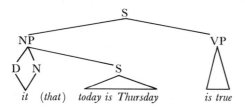

We must delete "it" unless we place "today is Thursday" after "true." Similarly, passive sentences may require "it." For example, we can say "I know that today is Thursday." This can be passivized to "That today is Thursday is known (by me)." This can be reordered to "It is known (by me) that today is Thursday." In the ordering of these transformations, it would appear that the deletion of "it" must come last. It is worth noting, by the way, that when the "that" clause follows a transitive verb, but almost never otherwise, the word "that" can be omitted. We can say "I know today is Thursday" but not "Today is Thursday is true." or "Today is Thursday is a fact." "It is true today is Thursday" seems of doubtful grammaticality.

Other constructions besides "that" clauses occur as S in noun phrases. Notice that these constructions seem to be used in much the same way as "that" clauses:

> For John to finish his work on time was hard.
> It was hard for John to finish his work on time.
> I expected John to finish his work on time.
> John's finishing his work on time surprised everybody.
> It surprised everybody John's finishing his work on time.
> I didn't anticipate John's finishing his work on time.

There are some important differences between these constructions and "that" clauses—deeper differences than are at first apparent. For example, we cannot say *"That John finished his work on time was hard." Instead of "hard" we could use such words as "true," "unexpected," "miraculous," and the like. These words are clearly comments on the *fact* that John finished his work on time. But the words that can replace "hard" in the sentence "It was hard for John to finish his work on time" are most typically manner words applicable to John's finishing his work, not to the *fact*. Thus we can say "difficult," "dangerous," "unusual," but not "true," "credible," or the like. We should also notice that the auxiliary of the sentence in which the so-called noun clause is embedded is different according to whether we choose a "for-to" or "that" sentence: we can say "For John to finish his work on time would surprise everybody" but not *"For John to finish his work on time surprised everybody."

Still another set of constructions often called noun clauses are those formed with question words such as "what," "who," "where," "when," and "why." These words are substitutes: they take the place of D – N in an unspecified noun phrase. It has often been pointed out that constructions with these words can be paraphrased by nouns followed by relative words, as in "I know what you're doing" and "I know that which you're doing." With "who" this is more difficult to apply: we can say "I know who you are" but not *"I know that who (or which?) you are." We could try substituting some general noun phrase such as "the person" or "the thing," but this would make these sentences very complicated. And if possible we would like to relate the "who" and "which" noun clauses to questions, which they obviously resemble, and to constructions with "whether" and "if," where no substitution seems to take place. The simplest explanation for all of these constructions seems to be the following: a main sentence containing a verb such as "know," "wonder," "ask," "discover," or "ascertain" may have an object consisting of "it" – S. (The set of copula-adjective constructions including "is clear," "is obvious," and the like as well as a few linking verbs ["become," "appear"] with the same adjectives may also have "it" – S subjects.) S in these constructions may be developed as Q (question) – S. Any NP of the embedded sentence may be developed as "who," "which," or "what," as the following diagram shows:

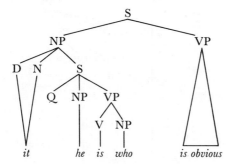

We have applied a transformation which converts the human noun in the embedded sentence to "who." We must still place "who" at the beginning of its clause (just as if it were a relative word) and delete "Q" and "it." This will give the string "Who he is is obvious." We could, of course, choose not to delete "it" and place the embedded sentence at the end: "It is obvious who he is."

In case we had chosen "if" or "whether" we would regard these as developments of "Q," in this way:

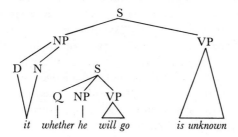

Once again we have two options: "Whether he will go is unknown" or "It is unknown whether he will go."

"Which" may be used in a different way from either an NP substitute or a Q substitute: notice that we can say not only "I know which he wants" but also "I know which book he wants." It seems difficult to avoid concluding that this "which" is a kind of demonstrative: it takes the place of phrases like "that" or "a certain." (Notice that the noun it accompanies may have other modifiers developed from sentences, as in "I know which red book—or which geology book—he wants." In the author's view, such sentences may be diagrammed in this way:

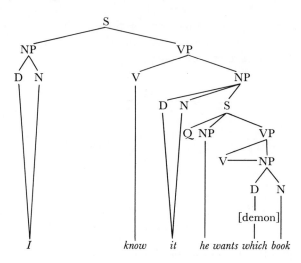

"It" must be deleted unless the sentence is passivized and reordered: "Which book he wants is known by me." "It is known (by me) which book he wants."

Adverb Clauses

We usually call clauses beginning with "when," "where," and the like adverb clauses. But, as we noted above, these words may be interrogative and they may also be relative as in "When are you going?" and "At the time when I met him. . . ." As interrogative words they occur in such indirect questions as "I know when you are leaving." This sentence must be contrasted to "I cry when you are leaving." It is clear that "when you are leaving" does two quite different things in these sentences: in the first it is the NP of the transitive verb "know." In the second it is only a time-phrase, analogous to "every morning." As Jacobs and Rosenbaum have pointed out (*English Transformational Grammar*, pp. 210–11), only the first permits the cleft-sentence transformation, which gives "What I know is when you are leaving." Only the second permits the adverb inversion transformation "When you are leaving, I cry." The same authors have suggested that clauses of this type can best be understood as relative clauses of the familiar type—but which modify deletable place and time words. We might diagram a sentence containing such a clause in this way:

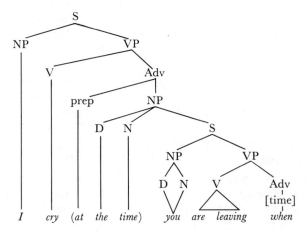

We must, of course, apply the relative word position transformation. We may optionally omit "at the time."

This analysis does not seem to account for clauses containing such words as "if," "because," "although," "unless," and the like. It may be that these words can be explained as derived from longer constructions containing the deletable relative word "that." For example, "if" might be read as "on the condition that," "because" as "for the reason that," "although" as "in spite of the fact that," and the like. These clauses need a great deal more study. At present, however, we can say with confidence that sentences may occur in adverb positions, that they have in general the same transposition privileges as adverbs, and that they are introduced by words typically used as substitutes for phrases like "at the time" and "in the place."

Conjoining

The most familiar and easily described sentence-combining process in English is conjoining. Conjoining involves nothing more than linking two or more sentences by "and," "but," "for," "either-or," or "neither-nor." Thus "She loved coffee" and "I loved tea" become "She loved coffee and I loved tea." Sometimes the same phrase occurs in both the conjoined sentences. In this case, we usually apply the identity-deletion transformation mentioned in other connections above. Thus the sentences "John likes Bessie" and "Bill likes Bessie" can become "John and Bill like Bessie." Similarly, the sentences "John likes Bessie" and "John likes Susie" can become "John likes Bessie and Susie." We can conjoin four sentences like this: "John likes Bessie; John likes Susie; Bill likes Bessie; Bill likes Susie"——▸"John and Bill like Bessie and Susie." If we had started with "John likes Bessie" and "Bill likes Susie" we could conjoin them only if we added the adverb "respectively": "John and Bill like Bessie and Susie, respectively."

It has often been observed that "and" is sometimes used to conjoin sentences which are not interchangeable with each other. Compare "She loved coffee and I loved tea" with "He started to drink and she divorced him." "And" not only links, it shows historical sequence; and if we reverse the order of the clauses in the second example we get a quite different story. "And" is used to show many other relationships, as these examples show: "You throw that and I'll call the police." ("If you throw that . . .") "You don't clean your room and I'll spank you." ("Unless you clean . . .") "He threw it and she called the police." ("Because he threw it . . .") "He built the house and they lived in it." ("After he built the house . . .") It is not clear at present just how these facts about "and" can be accounted for. But they seem to relate to the concepts of the nonrestrictive clause and to what we may wish to call the reduced adverbial clause.

Compare these sentences:

> The man listening to the radio is my brother.
> The man, listening to the radio, failed to hear the siren.

Notice that the first is *not* just another way of saying: "The man is listening to the radio and he is my brother." On the contrary, it says something like "You can identify the man as my brother by the fact that he is listening to the radio." The phrase "listening to the radio" is part of the phrase containing "the man" and it serves to identify the man. The second example, on the other hand, can be paraphrased as "The man was listening to the radio and he failed to hear the siren." It is certainly not a way of saying "You can identify the man who failed to hear the siren by the fact that he is listening to the radio." The second seems to be a kind of conjoined sentence with all the repeated material deleted. But notice that it is conjoined in a special way: it is a conjoining with an adverbial sense, and if the two clauses were independent, their order could not be changed. It paraphrases "Because the man was listening to the radio, he failed to hear the siren." Notice also that the second sentence permits the order "Listening to the radio, the man failed to hear the siren." This capacity for rearrangement is characteristic of adverbials in English.

The first sentence is an example of a reduced restrictive clause. As we saw, it comes from "The man who is listening to the radio is my brother." The second is what we usually call a nonrestrictive clause. It also may have the form "who is listening to the radio." Such nonrestrictive clauses are common, especially after proper nouns, as in "John, who is a Swede, hates the snow." But the clause "who is a Swede" certainly doesn't identify John. It provides nothing more than conjoined information. Notice that it may be reduced to "John, a Swede, hates the snow." Notice also that its position in the sentence may be changed: "A Swede, John hates the snow." This sentence, however, has at least the possible interpretation "Because he is a Swede, John hates the snow." In the author's opinion, we have this situation: Sentences may be conjoined. In case they contain a repeated noun, one may become a nonrestrictive modifier of the repeated noun in the other. This may be developed into a "who" or "which" clause (never a "that" clause) in which case it must remain in the usual position of a noun-modifying clause. But it may simply undergo the deletion of the repeated NP. When this occurs, the reduced clause may occur preceding as well as following the repeated NP. If it precedes it will have not just the additive meaning of "and," but rather one of its adverbial meanings. It is interesting that some of the same relations which we saw could be expressed by "and" can be expressed by these reduced sentences:

> Having completed his work, John went home. (When he had . . .)
> Dressing so carelessly, you'll never get a job. (If you . . .)
> Not eating wisely, you'll get sick. (Unless you . . .)

This much seems certain: that there is considerable similarity between so-called nonrestrictive modifiers and conjoined sentences. Conjoined sentences may be related causally, temporally, conditionally, and the like. The same thing is true of sentences containing nonrestrictive modifiers. The latter seem to be explained most simply as derived from conjoined sentences with an adverbial relation to the larger sentences they form part of.

Rearranging Sentence Parts

We have already illustrated several rearrangements of the parts of English sentences: we have shown that "it-S" constructions can have the order "it – main sentence – embedded sentence" or the order "embedded sentence – main sentence" with the deletion of "it." We have shown that adverb clauses can occur following a VP, between an NP and a VP, or preceding an NP. We have shown that nonrestrictive structures can either precede or follow NP's. We will discuss only two other optional rearrangements: the passive and the "there"-inversion.

The passive has already been mentioned and it is quite familiar. Certain verbs permit an object NP (or NP's) to become their subjects. When this occurs, a new auxiliary word is added. The original subject becomes the object of a "by"-phrase. Thus "Gentlemen prefer blondes" becomes "Blondes are preferred by gentlemen." The underlying structure:

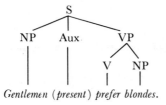

Gentlemen (present) prefer blondes.

is rearranged in this way:

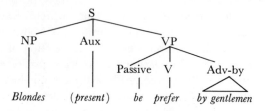

We must still apply the affix transformations which convert "be" to "are" and "prefer" to "preferred." The passive marker "be" must be attached to the auxiliary (though it originates as a feature of the verb) so that we can form the negation "Blondes are not preferred" and the question "Are blondes preferred?" The passive transformation may also be applied to sentences with indirect objects: We can say "John gave the cat to Bessie" and "The cat was given to Bessie by John." We can also say "John gave Bessie the cat" and "Bessie was given the cat by John." We seem to be using the rule that the NP immediately following a verb with the passive option may be placed in the position of the subject NP. (That is, we must place "to Bessie" immediately after the verb, deleting "to," if we are to produce "Bessie was given the cat by John.") It should be pointed out that "get" is a very common alternative form for the passive auxiliary: "He got run over by a truck." "Get," however, seems not to occur with verbs which have indirect objects. We do not say *"He got sold the car" or *"She got given diamonds."

The "there"-inversion is illustrated by sentences such as these: "There were ten people in the room," "There was a mouse under the bed." These can be viewed as focus-shifting transformations of "Ten people were in the room" and "A mouse was under the bed." This transformation is often used, however, in constructions without a place adverbial: we can say "There is no excuse for your behavior" or "Once there was a little old woman." We could not say "No excuse is for your behavior" nor "A little old woman was once." English has adapted what was originally only a way of expressing location (as in "There he goes") to serve the same purpose as German "es gibt" or French "il y a." Thus there is a rule in English that when the copula "be" occurs without one of its regular completers (an NP, an adjective, certain prepositional phrases, or a verb form) the "there"-inversion must be applied.

Simple, Complex, and Compound

School grammar commonly classifies sentences as simple, complex, and compound. These are usually defined as follows: simple sentences are those which contain only one subject and one predicate (either or both may be compound). Complex sentences are those which contain only one main, or independent sentence, and one or more modifying sentences. Compound sentences are those which contain at least two main, or independent, sentences. By now it should be clear that this is not a very satisfactory means of classification. According to these rules, the following sentences would both be classified as simple: "The dog disappeared" and "The dog, having attracted the affection of both the children living in the house of the man from Cuba, disappeared, leaving not a single trace behind." This would also be called a simple sentence: "A man from Mars and a man born on the earth would both share the characteristics of fearing death and loving life, however easy the first or hard the second." That is to say, our traditional definitions do not allow for the possibility of deleting parts of embedded or conjoined sentences. As a result, the definitions are somewhat arbitrary. They do not put into the same class sentences which are alike in important ways. Even when they are used as terms in rhetoric, they are not very useful when they are defined in the ordinary way. It is not true in any sense that I know of that sentences which contain only reduced embedded sentences are simpler than those which contain unreduced ones. Yet the school rhetorics do have an important point to make when they say such things as "Mature writing is characterized by having more complex sentences and fewer simple ones." It is true, as students of style have often pointed out, that formal written English has few sentences which consist only of an unmodified D – N and an unmodified VP. Furthermore, many studies of children's language have shown that such language is characterized by its large proportion of so-called compound sentences. But it seems to be true that only certain kinds of simple and compound sentences are marks of immaturity. For example, introductory sentence modifiers (whatever kind of sentence they may be attached to) seem to characterize a sophisticated style. The use of full rather than reduced relative clauses seems to characterize a formal, written style rather than a casual, spoken one. This aspect of English grammar needs much further study. But it seems clear that the ordinary use of the terms "simple," "complex," and "compound" does not tell us much that is useful about English sentences. It should be clear that the English language allows us to make a large number of predications within the surface form of a simple sentence, and that complex and compound sentences may in one sense be simpler than simple ones because they make the grammatical relations between their parts more explicit.

A Note on Deriving Sentences

It should be emphasized that when strings are said to be derived from each other or to precede or follow each other in a sequence of transformations no assertion is being made about the psychology of sentence construction. Sentence production is still very much a mystery. While we may observe ourselves in the process of composition trying out various alternative phrasings for the same predication, we do not want to assert that this must be carried out in a particular order or even that it takes a form at all like what is described above. What we have shown is relations among sentences—we have shown that the surface structure of sentences can be explained in a purely grammatical sense as deriving from a deep structure that may appear quite different. We have shown that sentences are more or less like each other in terms of their hypothetical derivations from deep structures. We are not making assertions about the nature of sentence production as it is carried on by actual speakers.

Topics for Investigation

1. Classify these sentences as "simple" or "complex" according to the school grammar rule which defines "complex" sentences as those having one or more subordinate clauses (each with its own subject and predicate) and "simple" sentences as those having only one subject-predicate sequence, regardless of the expansion of either part.

   a. I know what you know.
   b. Any rapidly moving motor-driven vehicle can cause these timid animals to flee for cover.
   c. Being a member of one of the old, aristocratic families, Ted yearns for a return to the days of proper respect for superior merit on the part of the genetically inferior people.
   d. Because he is a member of that family, Ted has a lot of pride.
   e. As a boy, he never behaved improperly.
   f. When he was in school, his marks were never above nor below "C."

2. What questions can you make up using these sentences as your basis:

   a. That year John was selling insurance to his friends in his old home town by knocking on doors and stopping passers-by.
   b. To keep body and soul together, John also worked in the campaign to make Peterson mayor.

3. Form the passives of these sentences. What similarities do they have as passives which they do not have as active sentences?

   a. The ignorant mob made Poltroon district attorney.
   b. Ned threw away all his money.
   c. To read the eulogy they obtained a judge.
   d. They couldn't account for their findings.

4. Combine these sentences in such a way that each clause is reduced as much as possible without losing any information:

> a. The yacht was driven by a motor. The yacht was manufactured in England. In England very fine craft are built. The yacht can make a speed of ten knots.
>
> b. John had exhausted his account. His account was for checking. John had tried every other avenue. John decided only one course was open to him. The course was this. He would pawn his mandolin. His father had brought him the mandolin from the Orient.

There are, of course, a great many more rules for the combination of basic strings and for optional basic transformations than those we have mentioned. You may find it interesting to expand the principles presented in this chapter by working out your own rules to account for these additional facts:

> a. Collect a list of postnominal modifiers smaller than relative clauses (e.g., prepositional phrases, verb forms, nouns, and adverbs). Do you find any that cannot be explained as reductions from relative-"be" constructions? What transformations might be used to explain those that do not appear to come from "be?"
>
> b. Are all relative clauses following proper nouns nonrestrictive? What specific features of a context (either in the same sentence or a preceding one) determine whether a relative clause is to be restrictive or nonrestrictive in form? Are there certain adjectives or determiners which, if they precede a noun, have the effect of making any following relative clause nonrestrictive?
>
> c. In school grammar, imperative sentences are often said to have "you" understood as the subject. But "you" as a noun of address can be added to any sentence: compare "You, shut the door" and "You, were you born in a barn?" Does an imperative have "you" understood in any other way than as a noun of address? If "you" is deleted, what would be the structure of the sentence from which the deletion is made?

Suggestions for Further Reading

This chapter is greatly indebted to the work of Roderick A. Jacobs and Peter S. Rosenbaum, *English Transformational Grammar* (Waltham, Mass.: Blaisdell Publishing Company, 1968). Some other works which have influenced it include J. F. Staal, "And," *Journal of Linguistics*, IV (April, 1968), 79–82; Andreas Koutsoudas, "On wh-words in English," *Journal of Linguistics*, IV (October, 1968), 267–73; Ralph B. Long, "Expletive *There* and the *There* Transformation," *Journal of English Linguistics*, II (March, 1968), 12–22; and Samuel J. Keyser, review of Sven Jacobson, "Adverbial Positions in English," *Language*, XLIV (1968), 357–73.

Three books mentioned in Chapter III provide a particularly good elementary discussion of transformations. These are Owen Thomas, *Transformational Grammar and the Teacher of English;* Paul Roberts, *English Syntax;* and Ralph Goodman in Norman C. Stageberg, *An Introductory English Grammar.* Three excellent books on a somewhat more advanced level are Emmon Bach, *An Introduction to Transformational Grammars* (New York: Holt, Rinehart & Winston, Inc., 1964); Andreas Koutsoudas, *Writing Transformational Grammars* (New York: McGraw-Hill Book Company, 1966); and Baxter Hathaway, *A Transformational Syntax* (New York: The Ronald Press Company, 1967). The reader should, of course, also consult the titles by Chomsky mentioned in the preceding chapter.

Robert B. Lees, *The Grammar of English Nominalizations* (Bloomington, Indiana: Research Center in Anthropology, Folklore, and Linguistics, Publication 12, Indiana University, 1960, rev. 1963) is still an illuminating account of the structure of English complex sentences.

Since nothing like a comprehensive, unified transformational grammar of English exists, the reader should also be aware of the journals which carry such studies. Some of the most important of these are *Language,* the journal of the Linguistic Society of America; the *International Journal of American Linguistics;* and *Journal of Linguistics,* the journal of the Linguistic Society of Great Britain.

The Uses of Grammar

CHAPTER 6 Now that we have had a brief look at the kinds of topics grammarians are concerned with and at the procedures they follow, it may be well to consider once again what grammar is for. As we noticed in Chapter II, it is necessary to distinguish between grammar as a scholarly study—the kind of study which has value as forming part of our common knowledge about the human race—and grammar as a school subject. It is the second use of grammar which we now want to consider in detail. The justification for teaching grammar in the schools usually takes one or the other of these forms: grammar is useful in helping children develop skill in using their native language, or grammar is one part of the general education which we should share if we are to be effective human beings. We want to consider the assumptions which underlie these justifications and the evidence which supports them.

Undoubtedly we are most familiar with the claim that students need to know grammar if they are to write grammatically—that is, if they are to avoid the mistakes in case and number and tense, in punctuation, and the like which seem to plague the beginning writer. But it is obvious that merely being able to assign grammatical names to the parts of sentences will not prevent ungrammaticality. If there is a relation between knowing grammar and avoiding errors in written English, it must involve something more than merely being able to analyze sentences. The errors of the beginning writer seem to have two main causes: major differences between the student's native dialect and standard English; and the fact that written English does not correspond in many respects to spoken English. So-called errors, such as "ain't," "he don't," "he talking," "he be talking," "growed," "he done it", are examples of forms which are perfectly grammatical in their proper regional and social setting. But these forms are rejected in serious written English. There is no doubt that an English program which is expected to enable children to communicate, especially in writing, outside their immediate circle of acquaintances, has to deal with the problem of dialect divergence. But what is involved here is essentially second-language learning, and it seems only reasonable that second-language learning techniques would be most effective. There is considerable agreement among language learning theorists at present that grammatical theory should have a minor place in second-language learning. No one now thinks that a student can master a new language merely by learning its grammatical rules. By far the largest share of the language student's time must be spent in drill, in sentence production and interpretation. Some language teaching specialists, in fact, recommend against requiring students to learn any generalizations about grammar at all. The goal of second-dialect teaching, like that of second-language teaching, must be the automatic production of grammatical sentences, and this kind of automatic control can come only after very large amounts of practice. It is certainly not true that a student can be said to have mastered the distinction between "don't" and "doesn't" when he is able to recite something like "third person singular present tense verb auxiliaries take the suffix -*es*."

It would be presumptuous to say, however, that grammar has no place in second-language or dialect learning. In the first place, the teacher must be very clear about what rules he wants his students to internalize, regardless of the fact that he may not wish the students to learn the rules in formal terms. There is considerable agreement that he needs to know the formal structure of both the students' native language and the one to be taught. He will thus be able to identify the points of greatest difficulty, be able to explain them in terms of a larger grammatical system, and be able to develop effective drills. For example, phrases in the pattern "I going" and "I be going" characterize American Negro dialect. These are not, as some teachers might suppose, accidental lapses. Rather they form part of an aspect system which has no exact counterpart in standard English. If children need to learn the standard forms, they will have to learn them in phrases which contain adverbials appropriate to the new verb phrase structures— otherwise the fact that a new way of expressing information about aspect will not be clear. Merely telling a child "Don't say 'I going'; say 'I'm going' or 'I go'" betrays the teacher's ignorance of the child's grammar and fails to provide the child with usable instruction. Thus it is clear that whether or not the child needs to be a grammarian, the teacher needs to be one.

It is by no means settled that the second-language or dialect learner is actually better off without explicit information about grammar. While a grammatical apparatus can easily get in the way of real language learning, it is a convenience to be able to use words such as "singular" and "plural," "present" and "past," and even to be able to say things like " 'Conduct' can be either a noun or verb depending on where you put the stress." There is also by no means complete agreement that language analysis is a useless activity in second-language learning. There seems to be a shift away from the view asserted very strongly a few years ago that language analysis serves no purpose at all. In summary, we can only say that while grammatical analysis clearly should not be the principal activity in the learning of a new language or dialect, we cannot say that it is useless. There seems to be a minimum body of formal grammatical information, including terminology for both classes and processes, which may actually contribute to the efficiency of language learning.

Regardless of the beginning writer's native dialect, he is certain to find that many features which characterize his spoken English are not acceptable in writing. For example, the structural and lexical ambiguity which we can tolerate in speech because we have a whole array of supplementary signaling devices—intonation, gestures, facial expressions, the physical context—cannot be tolerated in writing. Furthermore, we have rather fixed expectations about the economy, focus, logic, sequence, and explicitness of written English, expectations different from those we have of speech. Writing has been taught in schools for a very long time for just this reason; it is not true that the kinds of sentences we learned to produce automatically in our earliest childhood are acceptable in print. A transcription of a tape recording of almost any dialogue or set of extended spoken remarks will immediately show some of these important differences: Spoken English tends to be more redundant than written English; that is, in conversations we accept false starts, repetitions which make only slight modifications of what has already been uttered, sometimes even extended remarks which are only paraphrases. Writing must be much more economical. Focus in spoken English often comes from the nonlinguistic context. In written English, on the other hand, we expect it to be signaled explicitly. It is for this reason that cleft sentences ("What we propose is that you should ..."), "it" inversions ("It cannot be disputed that ..."), object transpositions ("Strontium 90 we take to be a product of ..."), and the like are more common in writing than in speech. Expressions signaled by "and" or simply by juxtaposition in spoken English must be related explicitly to their linguistic context in written English. We would say "He started to drink and his wife divorced him," but we would be more likely to write "When he started to drink, his wife divorced him." In addition, for no particular semantic reason, we expect to read—but not to hear—introductory participle phrases, appositives, and extended parentheses. Thus it is clear that written English is in many grammatical respects different from spoken English. Many of the topics of school grammar are introduced specifically to deal with the set of problems this fact introduces. For example our terms "complex sentence," "subordinate clause," "parallel construction," "introductory participle phrase," and the like reflect their common use in rhetorical as well as grammatical contexts. The problem here is quite different from that of the second-dialect learner. We are not asking students to learn rules which will compete with those they learned thoroughly and unconsciously in very early childhood. Rather we are asking them to select more frequently and more deliberately constructions which although familiar do not occur to them immediately as desirable alternatives to more colloquial ways of phrasing their ideas. We are asking them to meet the expectations of a wholly

unfamiliar audience—an audience at once more demanding and less re-
sponsive than those they have communicated with all their lives. It is partly
to meet these new demands that English teachers have provided their
students with a grammatical apparatus—a means of talking about the ways
in which a good written style can be distinguished from a bad one, or even
from a good spoken one. Research into the ways of teaching written style
is not at all conclusive. No one seriously claims, for example, that being able
to identify subordinate clauses and to subclassify them as adjective, noun,
or adverb makes a student a better writer. But there is something to be said
for being able to phrase, quickly and easily, several different ways of saying
the same thing. At least one ability of a good writer is that he can quickly
recognize what transformational possibilities are inherent in a given predication or series of them. There are no research findings to support the
claim that good writers are generally good grammarians; and a little reading
in linguistics will show that good grammarians are not always good writers.
But the intriguing possibility remains that a writer can improve his skill in
sentence production by going through deliberate processes of sentence
rephrasing. Two research studies which showed that students' skill in
sentence combining was increased by practice based on transformational
rules are described at the end of the chapter. Neither study claims that
the students' taste was improved; only that they could in general produce
a greater variety of sentences characteristic of written English than would
have been likely without the program.

Again, it seems clear that it is more important for the teacher to be
a grammarian than for the student to be one. The teacher needs to be able to
give a student much more explicit advice than that his sentences are "awk-
ward," "vague," "monotonous," "clumsy," and the like. He needs to be
able to make specific suggestions—suggestions not only for rephrasing
particular sentences but for modifying a whole style. He needs to able to show
a student how sequences of conjoined sentences can be improved through
embedding and deletion, how ambiguity can be cleared up through the use
of function words, how rhythm can be improved by the rearrangement of
modifiers, and so on. And he needs to know how to make up practice
materials which make principles like these more nearly automatic. This is
not to say that the teaching of writing can possibly consist mainly of practice
in sentence making; on the contrary, it must include extensive experience
with good essays, it must involve good conversation, it must be related to
topics the student can see are worth discussing. But it seemingly must also
include attention to the alternative forms sentences may take, a topic
which involves skill in recognizing the grammatical structure of sentences
and their transformations.

The claim that grammar is an essential part of a student's general
education takes several forms. It was mentioned above that grammatical
terms constitute part of ordinary English and that we have much the same

use for them that we have for terms like "radiation," "mass," "original sin," or "the negative income tax." That is, they are terms which, while they form part of the apparatus of the scholar, have become part of our ordinary way of talking about things. It is not necessary to assume, of course, that the schools have any obligation to teach this terminology. We can argue that people who need to know words can look them up. But this opens up the much larger question of what schools are for and even whether they should exist. If we assume that part of the school's task is linguistic—that is, to assist the child to acquire a sufficient command of our language so that he can without great handicap read, hear, and discuss the topics reasonably literate people generally read, hear, and discuss, then a case can be made for including the language of grammar in his general education. But there is less agreement among grammarians than there is among, say, chemists or economists as to what the language of their field is. Some schoolbooks have abandoned terms like "noun" and "verb" altogether and mention instead "Class I words" and "Class II words." Others use the familiar terms but define them in unusual ways. It is also not at all certain how much of the terminology of grammar can be called part of the word stock of literate English speakers. One could hazard a guess that it would include the names of the traditional parts of speech together with such terms as "singular," "plural," "sentence," "phrase," "clause," "present tense," "past tense," "passive," and perhaps a few others. But the subject needs to be much further studied. We can only say that the student who knows no grammatical terminology whatever will certainly be handicapped in interpreting much that he will be expected to read and hear.

The claim is sometimes made that the study of grammar helps "train the mind." The claim obviously is very similar to the one which used to be made for geometry—that it provided habits of thought or mental skills that could be transferred to other subjects. Thus however useless geometry turned out to be, it was worth learning just for the brain power it developed. This claim has been disputed for many years, and it has fallen into such disrepute that geometry itself is disappearing from the school curriculum. And whatever special abilities are supposedly transferrable from the study of grammar to other studies remain to be identified. Before we reject the whole ideas as pure nonsense, however, we need to ask whether we have phrased as fairly as possible the position of those who claim that grammar in some way trains the mind.

Logic is a subject which has been part of school curricula for literally thousands of years. It has recently been pushed up into the college curriculum, though it survives in high school programs in disguised forms such as "semantics" or "communication." During the last five years there has been renewed recognition of the importance logic can have in a good composition program. Two books have appeared which show how symbolic logic can be applied to specific composition tasks, and several experiments in applied logic have shown good results. The claim for logic is that it provides a symbolic structure which, applied to any set of ideas, permits the explicit identification of their logical relations. It identifies fallacious arguments and shows how arguments may be correctly structured. This is quite different from the vague claims which used to be made for geometry. The logicians provide not mental calisthentics but rather an explicit framework for the display of ideas. To the extent that grammar shares this characteristic with logic, it can make the same claim. For example, the tree diagrams showing how adverb phrases relate at different levels to the tree which represents the Verb Phrase (pp. 43–44) are making an assertion about the meaning of the entire sentence. The problems of apparent structural synonymity with different underlying relations and of structural difference with the same underlying relations are problems of interpretation which an adequate grammar can resolve. That is, grammar provides an apparatus for identifying underlying relations among the parts of sentences which is in many respects like that of logic. The difference is that the apparatus of grammar is concerned with its own sets of topics. It will not do, therefore, to say that grammar does not in any sense "train the mind." It can provide a sharper, more clearly structured way of identifying the relations which hold between the parts of sentences and is thus at least a potential tool in sentence interpretation and evaluation. It is particularly in the interpretation of literature that thinking like a grammarian may turn out to be helpful. Notice the first lines of Hopkins' "Spring and Fall":

> Márgaret, are you gríeving
> Over Goldengrove unleaving?
> Leáves, líke the things of man, you
> With your fresh thoughts care for, can you?

Hopkins clearly expects his reader to be a creative grammarian. He wants him to identify the underlying predications "Goldengrove is unleaving." "Question: Are you, Margaret, grieving over that?" "(Someone) cares for the things of man." "Question: Can you, with your fresh thoughts, care for leaves like that?" Hopkins expects the reader to recognize in the first sentence an embedded gerundive. In the second he wants us to find two principal inversions: object preceding subject; and what might be called a pseudo tag question analogous to "Walk in my flower beds, will you?" Furthermore, he wants us to recognize that "unleaving" is formed on the derived verb "leave" (i.e., sprout leaves), and that it is put together on the analogy of "undressing," "unbuttoning," etc. That is, it is a verb of the class sharing the general meaning "cyclic or repeated activity; capable of recurring." The reader without a strong sense of the transformational alternatives of Hopkins' sentences may very well be at a loss to get even what I. A. Richards called their plain sense. Thus skill in interpretation depends in part on the ability to identify the grammatical structure of sentences.

Any claim that grammar constitutes a legitimate part of a general education program must rest finally on the general relevance of grammar itself. It must be shown that scholarship in grammar has produced worthwhile results, that grammar is actually related to a wide range of other consequential studies, and that together with these other studies grammar can provide intellectual equipment useful enough to justify its cost in time and effort. These are questions that must be settled on intuitive rather than on logical grounds. Beyond reading, writing, and arithmetic, we can only guess which will prove most useful among the array of subjects making competing claims on the time of young students. Grammar—particularly a grammar which focuses on sentence building rather than sentence analysis —makes a strong claim for part of that time. For the teacher who finds grammar itself fascinating and who sees its relation to the whole study of communication which must be a central concern of education, the teaching of grammar is sufficiently justified. But we must recognize that the kind of pedestrian, dogmatic grammar most of us experienced as elementary school children has not proved very useful. It seems clear that if grammar is to have the relevance which would justify including it in the lower school curriculum, then it must be taught as a human subject—a subject which sheds light not only on sentences but on the human mind and on the behavior of human beings as members of society. It must be taught as the fascinating subject it can be—a subject which combines the elements of puzzle solving and artistic creation. It must be taught as one aspect of our continuing inquiry about ourselves—about what makes us human beings and how we manage to get information from one mind to another. It must be related to the problem of failure of communication—of interference from dialect or style or sentence choice in our attempts to bridge the space that separates us as individuals and members of groups. We can no longer defend the lifeless, irrelevant kind of grammar which our schools have traditionally offered.

Suggestions for Further Reading

On the relation of sentence analysis to second-language teaching, see Wilga M. Rivers, *The Psychologist and the Foreign Language Teacher* (Chicago: University of Chicago Press, 1964), especially pp. 115–30 and by the same author, *Teaching Foreign Language Skills*, (Chicago: University of Chicago Press, 1968). The reader should consult *Research in Education*, Educational Resources Information Center, U. S. Department of Health, Education, and Welfare for a listing of the large number of recent studies on second-dialect teaching. I. A. Richards, *Interpretation in Teaching* (New York: Harcourt, Brace & World, Inc., 1938) has much to say about the current debate over the place of grammar in the lower school curriculum. *Logic for Argument* by Jack Pitt and Russell Leavenworth (New York:

Random House, Inc. 1968) is an introductory text which relates modern logic to writing. *Transformational Sentence Combining: A Method for Enhancing the Development of Syntactic Fluency in English Composition*, the final report of a research program conducted by the Graduate School of Education, Harvard University, indicates that students using a transformational approach showed significant improvement in sentence-producing skills. The report, C. R. P. No. 5–7418, prepared by John C. Mellon, can be obtained from the Publications Office, Longfellow Hall, Appian Way, Cambridge, Massachusetts 02138. A similar project report prepared by D. R. Bateman and F. J. Zidonis may also be of interest. It is *The Effect of a Knowledge of Generative Grammar Upon the Growth of Language Complexity* (Columbus: Ohio State University, 1964), C. R. P. No. 1746, Office of Education, U. S. Department of Health, Education, and Welfare.

A Transformational Syntax by Baxter Hathaway (New York: The Ronald Press Company, 1967), provides a thorough discussion of some of the transformations of English and their relation to English composition. Hathaway avoids the elaborate formal symbolism which many teachers find difficult. *Transformational Grammar and the Teacher of English* by Owen Thomas, mentioned above, can also be recommended.

The relation of grammatical study to composition has been discussed rather fully by Albert H. Marckwardt in "Linguistics and English Composition," *Language Learning*, xi (March, 1961), 15–23; by Paul Roberts in "The Relation of Linguistics to the Teaching of English," *College English*, xxxii (1960), 1–9; and by Bertrand Evans in "Grammar and Writing," *Educational Forum*, XXIII (1959), 215–28. A recent study which proposes applications of grammar to composition teaching is Philip H. Cook, "Putting Grammar to Work: The Generative Grammar in the Generative Rhetoric," *English Journal*, LVII (1968), 1168–75. The reader may also find interesting the study by William R. Slager, "Effecting Dialect Change Through Oral Drill," *English Journal*, LVI (1967), 1166–76. Francis Christensen has given a very clear and convincing statement of the limitations on the usefulness or grammar in composition in his article "The Problem of Defining a Mature Style," *English Journal*, LVI (1968), 572–79. A similar and very carefully researched argument appears in James Moffett, *Teaching the Universe of Discourse* (Boston: Houghton Mifflin Company, 1968), Ch. 5.

For a discussion of the theory and procedures for presenting concepts inductively, see Hilda Taba and Freeman F. Elzey, "Teaching Strategies and Thought Processes," *Teachers College Record*, LXV (1964), 524–34.

Sounds and Letters
in American English

CHAPTER 7 Languages are first of all ways of communicating through sounds. This chapter will attempt to provide a way to describe the sounds of English systematically. It will in addition attempt to show what relation these sounds bear to the English writing system, a subject which has repeatedly aroused controversy throughout the history of the study of the teaching of reading and spelling.

It is remarkable that although the facts about the sounds and letters of English and the relationships that hold between them are ascertainable, the controversy about phonics and its place in reading and spelling programs has been based mostly on opinions about how well children used to read or on ill-derived statistics about the percentage of "phonetically" spelled words in English. It is not the intention of this chapter to go into the complicated topic of the psychology of reading; it will be sufficient to say that it is assumed that reading is deriving from a printed page the same kinds of information one obtains from listening to speech. The beginner learns to read by finding on the page words and grammatical constructions which are already part of his spoken language; as he becomes more skilled, he may expand his command of spoken language from what he has learned by reading. It is clear that writing is a way of transmitting *language*. For the normal speaker language involves primarily speaking and listening skills which are already highly developed before he begins to read. When he learns to read, he is only learning to respond to a different kind of signal, not learning language as such. Approaches to reading that claim to lead the child directly from the written symbol to its meaning, seemingly bypassing the language the child already knows, present an unnecessarily formidable task and one closely resembling foreign language learning. Learning that a particular black mark on a page represents "a small, lithe, soft-furred animal, domesticated, etc . . ." seems immeasurably more difficult than learning that *c*, *a*, and *t*, stand for his familiar phonemes /k/, /æ/, and /t/ and that they combine to form the equally familiar word "cat." It follows that the more closely reading materials can be related to the spoken language the child already commands, the more efficiently he can go about learning the new set of signals. It must be emphasized that we are talking about the earliest stages of learning to read. Skilled readers do not "sound out" familiar words—but even they can add to their reading vocabulary by relating printed letters to sounds.

It is, then, of the utmost importance to find out what relationships there are between the sounds and letters of English and how this relationship can be exploited in leading children to respond to written as well as spoken language. Contrary to what most school pupils are accustomed to, the discussion must begin with the sounds rather than the letters. A moment's consideration of the history of English spelling will show why this is true: the sound *system* of English, despite permutation, additions, and losses, has had an uninterrupted development from prehistoric times. It has maintained much the same consonant system with rather considerable, but systematic, variations, particularly in the vowels, throughout the historical period. But the spelling system of English has undergone erratic modifications, the most serious being the imposition of numerous continental spellings and the loss of many phonetically happy Old English ones following the Norman conquest. Examples are *th*, *gh*, and *wh*, all representing sounds spelled less ambiguously in Old English. Further distortions were caused by the spelling habits of the continental printers who practiced their craft in England in the fifteenth and sixteenth centuries, by scholars determined to preserve and restore classical spellings, and, most important of all, by the development and widespread use of "standard" spellings imposed by dictionaries and schoolmasters. These "standard" spellings have tended to be arbitrary and sacrosanct. While sound change has proceeded at a seemingly constant rate, spelling has changed very little since the seventeenth century.

In addition, it hardly needs to be pointed out that no native speaker learns the sound system of English by sounding out letters; he learns it by listening and by making sounds, first at random, later systematically. We can thus take the sounds as our point of departure, recognizing the fact that the spelling system is in some respects unsystematic and unpredictable, and does not necessarily reveal very much about the current state of English as a language.

The question "what are the sounds of English?" ought to have a simple answer; any normal five-year-old can distinguish "pat" from "bat," "bat" from "but," "but" from "bun," and so on through twenty or more consonant contrasts and anywhere from seven to twelve vowel contrasts. We should be able, then, to say something like: there is the sound "b," the sound "t," etc. Unfortunately the matter is much more complicated than this. Certain sounds have considerable variation in different phonetic environments, so much that it is difficult to determine which other sounds they might be classified with or whether they constitute separate sounds. Consider the "t" and "d" of western American *petal* and *pedal*: are they different sounds, the same sound (if so, are both "t" or both "d"?), or some other sound entirely, say "r"? Probably the most accurate way to deal with the whole problem is to make an inventory of the distinctive sound features—such as voicing and voicelessness, nasality and orality—and to describe, preferably in acoustical terms, the pronunciation of a given word as the simultaneous or sequential occurrence of these features. For example, it is clear that a word such as "bin" is not broken into segments such as /b/, /i/, and /n/. The features of voicing and laxness are sustained throughout the word. The feature of orality is sustained until the onset of /n/. At the onset of /i/, the feature of consonantality gives way to vocality. A chart will show how the sound features that make up the word overlap the segments which our preoccupation with spelling leads us to expect.

	b	*i*	*n*
Vocalic	−	+	−
Consonantal	+	−	+
Interrupted	+	−	−
Nasal	−	−	+
Lax	+	+	+
Voiced	+	+	+

Other features could, of course, be mentioned, but that would involve an elaborateness of terminology and a degree of preparation in phonetics far beyond the requirements of this discussion. We shall instead adopt an approach long found useful in practical descriptions and in the construction of efficient alphabets, an approach called "phonemic analysis."

This approach appears to underlie all the traditional alphabets (as opposed to syllabaries, such as Japanese katakana, or logographic systems, such as Chinese). It is based in general on the principle of writing a separate character to represent each new combination of distinctive sound features. Thus even though all the other features remain the same, if a feature such as voicing is introduced and that feature is distinctive in the language in question, a new character is written. The procedure by which the phonemes of a given language may be identified is somewhat as follows: it is the case that while it is almost impossible for anyone to say a word in precisely the same way twice, somehow we do repeat words. That is, we notice the similarities and ignore the differences between two pronunciations of the same word. We can set up rough-and-ready units of sound by exploiting this principle: if native speakers regard two pronunciations as the same, we can say those pronunciations consist of the same units of sound; if they regard them as different, we can say that at least one unit of sound is different. If the native speaker considers "but" and "but" the same and "but" and "cut" different, he has provided data for identifying at least two phonemes of English. The process of phonetic analysis consists of experimenting with minimal pairs, that is, pairs that are as little different from each other as possible, to determine which units of sound feature native speakers consistently identify as different. Typically such facts as the effect of neighboring sounds on a given sound as well as the effects of stress and position to the beginnings and ends of words are considered. Such tests show that, for example, the aspiration (puff of breath) that accompanies initial "p" is not significant in English, since native speakers would not typically regard the pronunciations [phut] (with aspiration) and [put] (without aspiration) as different words. Thus a unit /p/, can be set up, contrasted to /t/, /d/, /k/, /g/, etc b.,ut not contrasted to [ph] (aspirated), [p'] (unreleased), etc. It will be clear that this approach is not particularly elegant from the methodological point of view. There is, for example, no infallible technique for segmenting strings of sounds: should the nasalization that accompanies, but seldom follows, the "r" of "aren't" be regarded as an occurrence of /n/, or should we say that English has a nasalized and an unnasalized /r/? Furthermore, the minimal pair test itself presupposes the identification of some unit such as the "word," and this may involve circularity, since the boundaries of words can usually only be identified after some phonological analysis has taken place. In addition, native speakers may disagree about whether they regard two pronunciations as realizations of two different words or of the same word. An example would be the doubtful status of [ž] finally. Are "rouge" and "garage" with final consonants pronounced more or less in the French way different from "rouge" and "garage" pronounced with the final consonant of "judge"? Despite these difficulties, the practicality of the phoneme concept has been demonstrated repeatedly by field linguists preparing descriptions and literacy materials. We shall therefore attempt to specify the phonemes of English: that is, the set of units which represent all the sound differences speakers of English actually use to distinguish one word from another.

The Consonant Phonemes

We shall make the traditional divison into separate vowel and consonant systems, despite the fact that in purely phonetic terms, the two systems form a continuum. Consonants are those sounds that are relatively close and nonresonant; vowels are open and resonant. Thus [p] is obviously a consonant and [a] a vowel; but such sounds as [w], [y], [l], and [r] are somewhere on the border between the two systems. The reasons for the division will become clear when we discuss the structure of the syllable. In addition, we shall follow the tradition in charting the phonemes according to their articulation.

The following terms may require explanation:

> *Stop:* articulated with momentary complete closure of the lips or the tongue and the inside of the mouth. All other consonants as well as the vowels are called *continuant.* E.g., /p/, /t/, /k/.

> *Fricative:* formed with near but incomplete closure, resulting in a rubbing sound. E.g., /f/, /s/.

Nasal: formed with air escaping through the nose. Sounds that are not nasal are *oral.* E.g., /m/ (nasal) as opposed to /p/ (oral).

Labial: formed with the lips. Bilabial sounds involve both lips; labiodental ones, the lower lip and upper teeth. E.g., /b/, /w/, /m/.

Dental: formed with the teeth in contact or near contact with the tongue. Interdental articulations involve placing the tip of the tongue between the teeth. E.g., *th* in "thin."

Alveolar: formed with the tongue in contact or near contact with the ridge above the upper teeth. E.g., /t/, and /d/.

Palatal: formed with the tongue in contact or near contact with the hard roof of the mouth. E.g., the *sh* of "ship."

Velar: formed with the tongue in contact or near contact with the soft palate at the back of the mouth. E.g., /k/ and /g/.

The units represented by the characters in the chart below appear to account for all the consonant contrasts in English. No character appears to be unnecessary. The reader can test this assertion by making up minimal sets such as *pot, bot, tot, dot, got, jot; chop, bop, top, cop,* etc. Some contrasts will occur in very few such sets; for example, there are few instances of contrast between the voiced and voiceless fricatives (/θ/ and /ð/, /š/ and /ž/, etc.) within words; /ž/ never occurs initially and very seldom finally (in some dialects, never); /ŋ/ never occurs initially; /h/ only occurs initially. But the set of characters given here nevertheless appears to represent all and only the consonant phonemes of English. It must be emphasized that the units here called "phonemes" do not represent exact occurrences of the same sound; rather they are cover terms for sets or ranges of sound contrasted to all other such sets; the members of any one set are not, in general, contrasted to each other. It must be further emphasized that this is a practical description, not an attempt to give a total accounting of the distinctive features of English; machines capable of measuring sound features accurately would undoubtedly show that the classes identified here do indeed sometimes overlap and that, on the other hand, quite dissimilar sounds have been grouped under the same phoneme. This does not, however, affect the practical usefulness of an analysis such as the one given here.

	Bi-labial	Labio-dental	Inter-dental	Alveolar	Palatal	Velar	Glottal
Stops							
Voiceless	p			t	*č	k	
Voiced	b			d	*j	g	
Continuants							
Fricative							
Voiceless		f	θ	s	š		h
Voiced		v	ð	z	ž		
Nonfricative							
Nasal	m			n			
Oral	w			l	r, y	ŋ	

*č and j are usually called affricates, that is, sounds made with a stop onset followed by friction. They are sometimes transcribed [tš] and [dž]. Sample words:

/p/	put	supper	stop	/š/	shoe	washer	lash
/b/	but	rubber	cub	/ž/		pleasure	rouge
/t/	top	butter	pot	/h/	hit		
/d/	dell	ladder	lad	/m/	miss	hammer	dam
/č/	chop	butcher	batch	/n/	no	linen	don
/ǰ/	Jim	legend	edge	/ŋ/		singer	sing
/k/	catch	packet	back	/w/	will		
/g/	go	beggar	leg	/l/	let	teller	sell
/f/	fat	loafer	off	/s/	sit	missing	pass
/v/	vat	lover	grove	/z/	zoo	losing	buzz
/θ/	thin	ether	lath	/r/	round	barrel	car
/ð/	that	leather	bathe	/y/	yet		

The Vowel Phonemes

The vowels of English are much more difficult to reduce to order than are the consonants. There are several reasons for this: the earliest records show that the various dialects of Old English had different vowel inventories, and traces of these ancient dialect divisions still exist. In addition, new dialects have emerged, also characterized in part by their vowel systems. Furthermore, within the same dialect areas at present some uncertainty about the phonemic status of vowels can usually be found. People from apparently identical regional and social backgrounds will frequently give different answers to such questions as whether "caught" and "cot" are homonyms, whether "gist" and "just" (adv.) have the same vowel, whether the vowel of "bait" is a simple vowel or a diphthong, and the like.

We shall use a traditional vowel chart, organized, like the consonant chart, on articulatory lines. The system represented here reflects central and western American usage. Only two sets of terms are required: high, middle, and low, with reference to the relative height of the most tense part of the tongue; and front, central, and back, referring to the relative vertical position of the most tense part of the tongue. The characters /w/ and /y/ indicate tension and diphthongization (or length). /w/ indicates diphthongization toward the back of the mouth, /y/ toward the front. The vowels are numbered to permit more convenient comment. Please note in the description that follows that / / enclose phonemic symbols and [ ] enclose subphonemic (phonetic) ones.

	Front	Central	Back
High	1. iy "bead"		8. uw "mood"
	2. i "bit"		9. u {a. "butch" / b. "foot"}
Mid	3. ey "laid"		10. ow "road"
	4. e "bet"	6. ə "but"	
Low	5. æ "bat"	7. a "bot"	11. ɔ {a. "off" / b. "bought"}

There are, in addition, the following common diphthongs:

12. ay "bite"   13. oy "boil"   14. aw "bout"

1. iy = "bead." This vowel commonly has a more tense, relatively short variant before voiceless consonants. Some analysts treat it as a unitary phoneme, usually written /i/. In such systems, (2) is written /I/.

2. i = "bit." This vowel (at least in central and western American English), like (4), (5), and (8) never occurs at the ends of words. This fact is relevant to the discussion of spelling which follows.

3. ey = "laid." For many speakers of English, this vowel, like (1) could be considered a unit, usually written /e/. In such systems, (4) is written /ɛ/.

5. æ. The vowel of "bat," "bath," "dance," "smash" and similar words differs considerably from one dialect area to another. British and New England English frequently have a centralized variant, or even [a], before the voiceless fricatives and [n]. Southern American English may have a palatalized, or fronted, diphthong [æy] in this position.

6. ə. The vowel of "but" is not here distinguished from the unstressed vowel of words like "sofa" and "about." For American English there appears to be no significant structural or phonetic reason for setting up another phoneme, say /ʌ/. For British English, the stressed and unstressed mid-central vowels are usually regarded as separate phonemes.

7. a. For many Americans, no distinction is made between "bot" and "bought," "cod" and "cawed," "dawn" and "don" and the like. Such speakers have a single, rather widely varying low central-back vowel phoneme.

8. uw = "mood." Like (1) and (3), this vowel is frequently short and tense especially before voiceless consonants. Some analysts symbolize it with /u/ and designate (9) as /U/.

9. u. This vowel comes into modern English from two principal sources, the "shortening" of historic /uw/ in such words as "foot" and "hook" (notice that in most words the *oo* spelling still represents /uw/) and from historic /u/ spelled *u*, as in "put" and "full." In discussions of spelling, vowels from the first source follow "long" vowel rules, those from the second, "short" vowel rules.

10. ow. The comment on (1), (3), and (8) also applies to this vowel. For some speakers, particularly New Englanders, the vowel of "road" or "home" is probably most accurately represented by a simple vowel /o/. If a speaker distinguishes "four" and "for," "mourning" and "morning," and the like, he needs both /ɔ/ and /o/ to represent his dialect. Otherwise, he probably does not.

11. ɔ. Like /u/, this vowel is from two principal sources, the historic diphthong /aw/, as in the late Middle English pronunciation of "bought" and "law," and historic "short o," as in "off," "log," and the like. Again, words from the first source follow "long" vowel rules, those from the second, "short" vowel rules.

Vowels (2), (4), (5), (6), (7), (9a), and (11a) will be called *short* vowels in the discussion that follows. The rest of the vowels, including the diphthongs will be called *long*. It should be emphasized that phonetically speaking (9a) and (9b) are the same, as are (11a) and (11b). They are separated here only because each has two common spelling variants, one which follows *long* vowel rules, and one which follows *short* ones. It should also be emphasized that while *length* and *shortness* do not describe very accurately how the two subsystems of English vowels are distinguished, there *are* two subsystems. One system, the so-called long vowels, is characterized in articulatory terms by greater tension and by diphthongization (which explains why these vowels are called *long*). The other system, the *short* vowel system, is characterized by lax articulation and by the absence of diphthongization. In structural terms, the long vowels can occur at the ends of words. The short vowels (with very few exceptions) cannot. This difference explains why the tradition has developed of "closing" syllables containing short vowels by adding a consonant letter. It also explains why vowels are almost always short before consonant clusters.

The words "few" and "mute" contain the sequence /yuw/, which is often called a long vowel. This nucleus is actually a combination of the consonantal /y/ and the vocalic /uw/. Although there is no particularly appropriate place for this sequence in the vowel chart, it must be considered along with the vowels in any discussion of spelling because it alternates in a regular way with /uw/.

An additional vowel which many investigators use is /ɨ/. This is a high central vowel which occurs for some speakers in such words as "just" (adv.), "will" (aux.), and "sister." For most American speakers the unstressed vowel before /z/ in "houses" and /d/ in "hated" is high central. Whether this unstressed vowel is ever contrasted to /ə/ is open to debate.

The Consonant and Vowel Letters

With twenty-four consonant phenomes and about fourteen vowel phoneme sequences, the English language can hardly be represented accurately with twenty-six letters. The most severe shortage will obviously be in the letters used to represent vowels, but at least four consonants will have to be represented by letters already used for other sounds. It is thus immediately obvious that no one-to-one correspondence exists between English sounds and letters. The writing system could, however, be relatively phonetic even without this correspondence if other devices, such as doubling or clustering were used—and, obviously, this has happened to some extent in the history of English spelling.

The tables below will show how closely our consonant system is represented in the vast majority of English words. Keep in mind that we are going from sound to spelling except where otherwise noted. The tables divide the consonants into three main classes, the doubling consonants, the nondoubling consonants, and the semivowels. The doubling consonants are those which are written with more than one character (e.g., *b* becomes *bb*, *k* becomes *ck*) after short vowels. The nondoubling consonants lack this characteristic. The semivowels are sounds which are consonant-like at the beginnings of syllables but vowel-like at the ends. It is important to notice that there are differences in the way English consonants are spelled at the beginning, the middle, and at the end of words. Spelling lessons which focus on sounds in isolation or on initial sounds only overlook some important regularities of our sound-letter system.

The Doubling Consonants

/p/, /b/, /t/, /d/, /k/, /g/, /f/, /s/, /m/, /n/, /l/, /r/, /č/, /ǰ/.

1. The following consonants are represented by double characters after the "short" vowels [(2), (4), (5), (6), (7), (9a), and (11a)] *within* words. Otherwise they are single.

/p/	pin	supper	stop	cf. super
/b/	bin	rubber	jab	cf. ruby
/t/	tin	latter	rat	cf. later
/d/	din	bidding	bad	cf. biding
/g/	get	buggy	rug	cf. bugle (Spelled *gh* in four common words.)
/m/	men	summer	rim	cf. humor (Spelled -*mb* in a few words.)
/n/	net	funny	fan	cf. finer (Spelled *gn*, *pn*, and *kn* in a short list class.)
/r/	run	furry	far	cf. fury

2. The following consonants are represented by double characters after the "short" vowels within *and at the ends of words*. Otherwise they are single.

/f/	fin	suffer	off	(Spelled *ph* in a few borrowed words and *gh* after *ou* in five common words.)
/l/	lip	bully	ball	
/k/	kin	packer	lock	(Note that double *k* is written *ck*.)

(Before the letters *a*, *o*, and *u*, /k/ is usually spelled *c*. The sound sequence /ks/ is spelled *x* in bases, not in base + suffix: cf. "box," "rocks." The sound sequence /kw/ is spelled *qu*. In consonant clusters, /k/ is *c* if it precedes another consonant.)

/s/ sip fussy pass

(Note that /s/ at the beginning of a morpheme may be spelled *c* before *e*, *i*, or *y*. Within a morpheme after a long vowel and before a vowel it is almost always spelled *c* and at the end of a word, *ce*. Cf. "city," "gracious," "face," "paste." It is spelled *ps* in a few borrowed words.)

/z/   zip   dizzy   fuzz

(Note that /z/ after a long vowel and before a vowel is almost always spelled *s* and at the end of a word *se*. Cf. "please," "laser.")

/č/   church   wretched   fetch

(Note that double *ch* is spelled *tch*. Cf. "each," "roach.")

/ǰ/   jump   ledger   ridge

(Note that double *j* is spelled *dg*. After long vowels, /ǰ/ is spelled *g* before vowels and *ge* at the ends of words. Cf. "rage," "wager.")

The Nondoubling Consonants

/v/, /ð/, /θ/, /s/, /z/, /h/, /w/, /y/.

1. The unitary characters.

/v/   vile   liver   drive

(Note that at the end of words /v/ is written *ve*. A few recent coinages show double *v*: "flivver," "revving.")

/h/   hat   unhappy

(Note that /h/ occurs only at the beginning of morphemes.)

2. The complex characters.

/θ/   thin   ether   bath

(Note that between vowels *th* representing /θ/ is extremely rare.)

/ð/   this   either   bathe

(Note that initial /ð/ spelled *th* is extremely rare. At the ends of words /ð/ is spelled *the*.)

/š/   ship   rasher   wash

(Note that in complex words with a base ending in /s/ and a suffix beginning with /i/ or /y/, the pronunciation is /š/ but the spelling remains *si* or *ci* as in "mission" and "gracious." "Sure" and "sugar" show common exceptional spellings of /š/.)

/ž/   pleasure   rouge

(Note that /ž/ does not occur initially. It occurs finally only in partially assimilated words of French origin. Medially it occurs when a base ends with /z/—usually from /d/—and a suffix begins with /i/ or /y/, as in "derision" and "decision." It can also be found in a few French borrowings spelled *su* as in "treasure.")

3. The semivowels.

/w/   will   power   plow

(Note that initially and after consonants /w/ is like the other consonants. Medially and finally, where it occurs as a vowel off-glide, it is spelled *w*, *u*, or sometimes *o* or *a* as in "cloud," "loaf," and "food." Its occurrence as an off-glide can best be considered with the discussion of the relevant vowels below.)

/y/   you   flyer   play

(Note that initially /y/ is like the other consonants. Medially and finally where it occurs as a vowel off-glide, it is spelled *y* or *i* or sometimes *e* or *a* as in "playing," "daily," "green," and "plead." /y/ occurs commonly between consonants and /uw/ where it is spelled *ew*, *u*, or *eu*. Its occurrence as an off-glide can best be considered with the discussion of the relevant vowels below.)

It is clear from Chart I that the spelling of English consonants shows a high degree of regularity. Only the spellings of /k/ and /s/, /s/ and /c/, /s/ and /z/, and /š/ and /ž/ involve real unpredictability, and even for these consonants there is unpredictability in only a few positions. The list of "irregular" spellings including words like "ghost" and "knight," "trough" and "rhyme" is so short as to be easily memorizable. G. B. Shaw's famous spelling for "fish"—*ghoti*—is, of course, in complete violation of English spelling rules. Whatever the faults of English spelling it is never the case that initial *gh* stands for /f/ or that final *ti* stands for /š/.

The irregularities the chart shows are explainable in historical terms, although this information may be of little comfort to a struggling speller. The *k-c-s* ambiguity results from the fact that in Old English all /k/'s were represented by *c*, while /s/ was represented by *s*. But under French influence, beginning before and continuing to some extent ever since the Norman conquest, words in which *c* stood for /s/ (from Latin /k/ before front vowels) were introduced. The letter *k*, which was included in most continental alphabets, came to be used no doubt principally to reduce the ambiguity resulting from having such pairs as the French "cell" and the Old English "cyll" (= "kill"). But *k* never completely replaced all Old English *c*'s and many new French words containing *c* for /k/ were also introduced. Thus we

CHART I. LETTERS REPRESENTING THE ENGLISH
CONSONANT PHONEMES

		Between Vowels		Word Final		In Same Morpheme		
Phoneme	*Morpheme Initial*	*After Long Vw*	*After Short Vw*	*After Long Vw*	*After Short Vw*	*Before Consn't*	*After Consn't*	*Common Exceptions*
/p/	p	p	pp	p	p	p	p	
/b/	b	b	bb	b	b	b	b	
/t/	t	t	tt	t	t	t	t	doubt, debt
/d/	d	d	dd	d	d	d	d	
/g/	g	g	gg	g	g	g	g	ghost, ghoul
/m/	m	m	mm	m	m	m	m	
/n/	n	n	nn	n	n	n	n	gnat, gnaw, know, knife
/r/	r	r	rr	r	r	r	r	rhyme
/f/	f	f	ff	f	ff	f	f	phil-, phon-, laugh, cough
/l/	j	l	ll	l	ll	l	l	
/k/	k-*i, e* / c	k	ck	k	ck	c	k	/kw/ → qu /ks/ → x
/s/	c-*e, i, y* / s	c*V* / s*C*	ss	ce	ss	s	s	
/z/	z	s(z)	zz	se(ze)	zz			was, has, is
/č/	ch	ch	tch	ch	tch		ch	fu*tu*re
/ǰ/	j	g	dg	ge	dge		ge	
/v/	v	v	v	ve	ve		v*V*	
/h/	h							
/θ/	th	th	th	th	th	th	th	
/ð/	th	th	th	the	the			
/š/	sh	t / c -i,y / s	t / c -i,y / s		sh	sh	sh	
/ž/		s -i,u	s -i,u	ge				
/w/	w						w	q*u*ick
/y/	y							
/ŋ/		ng	ng	ng	ng	n		

C stands for consonant or consonant cluster.
V stands for vowel.

have both *k* and *c* (before back vowels) representing /k/ and both *s* and *c* (before front vowels) representing /s/.

Other difficulties, such as the fact that the syllable /čər/ can be spelled either *ture* or *cher* or that /šən/ can be spelled either *tion, sion,* or *shun* have a similar history. They represent borrowings from French which retain their French spellings but are homophonous with Old English syllables with regular spellings. Fortunately, most such irregular spellings are only irregular from a purely phonemic point of view. They are quite regular given another

CHART II. LETTERS REPRESENTING THE ENGLISH VOWEL
PHONEMES BASED ON THE THORNDIKE WORD LIST OF 3000
MONOSYLLABLES

Phoneme	Over 200 (Examples)	100-200	50-100	10-50	Before /r/	Initial	Final	Special Environments	Common Exceptions
/i/	i					i			build, guilt, been
/e/	e		ea			e			said
/ə/	u				e	u, i(6), u(8)		*worC*(7), *ough*(3)	blood, flood, were, was, learn, pearl, (See note 1.)
/æ/	a					a			plaid
/a/	o				a	o	a	*waC*	heart
/ɔ/			o		o	o	aw	*alC*, *ough*(8), *augh*(3)	broad
/u/			u	oo					w, sh, c } *ould*
/iy/	ee, ea			eCe	ee, ea	ea	ee, ea, e(5)	*ield*(4)	ski, seize, key
/ey/	aCe, ai/y			ei/y	a-e, ai, ea	a	ay	*eigh*	there, where, great, break
/uw/		oo, u-e			oo		ew, oo(3), ue(6)	*ough*(2)	shoe, who, do, you, flu
/ow/	oCe	oa	ow		o-e, oa(5)	o, oa(5)	ow, o(3), oe(6)	*ough*(2), *ost*(4), *old*(10)	own, sew
/ay/	iCe				i-e	i	ie(5), igh(4), y	*ind*(5), *ild*(3), *ight*(14)	guy, buy
/oy/		oi/y				oi	oy		
/aw/			ow, ou		ou	ou	ow	*ough*(2)	
/yuw/				uCe	u-e	u	ew, ue(6)		feud, view

Numerals in ( ) show number of occurrences in the Thorndike list.

C stands for consonant or consonant cluster.

[1] /ə/ is often spelled *o* before *m*, *n*, and *v* as in *come, some, dove, love, done, ton, one, won,* and *son.*

principle of English spelling, that morphemes in general retain their basic spelling regardless of changes in pronunciation. This principle will be discussed below. But the spelling of the vowels will have to be discussed first.

It was noted above that the vowel sounds of English show much more dialect variation than do the consonants. This tendency to change also affects the spelling of the vowels, since spelling tends to lag behind sound change. As a consequence, the spelling of the vowels creates many more difficulties for the learner. There are relatively few vowel sounds that are spelled with anything like complete regularity (/i/ spelled *i* is the best example); but for every vowel sound, some spellings are "better guesses" than others. Chart II shows the factors that must be considered in the choice of a vowel spelling and the spellings that are most probable in English monosyllables. It is clear from the chart that the short vowels /i/, /e/, /æ/, and /ə/ are spelled most predictably. Each shows over 200 regular spellings and relatively few exceptions. The vowels /a/, /u/, /oy/, /iy/, /uw/, /ay/, /aw/, and /yuw/ have two principal spelling variants. Only /ey/, /ɔ/, and /ow/ show three or more common spellings. Even these irregularities are more predictable than they may seem: *ai* and *ay* representing /ey/ and *oi* and *oy* representing /oy/ are selected according to the rule that *i* occurs within words, *y* at the end. Similarly, *aw*, *ow*, and *ew* occur at the ends of words instead of their variants with *u*. But no amount of explaining will spare the learner the trouble of memorizing the vowel spellings of "beat" and "beet," of "read" and "red," and similar words. Some very general principles which every good speller must be aware of include the following:

1. "Short" vowels are almost always spelled with single characters.

2. "Long" vowels are almost always spelled with multiple characters. (It is a serious mistake to lead children to regard the "long" sound as the normal sound of the vowel letters. The "short" sound is the normal sound. The "long" sound is always related to vowel letter *sequences*.)

3. Final (postconsonantal) *e* is *never* silent; it serves as part of a long vowel graph (e.g., i-e, o-e, e-e, a-e, u-e) or as a consonant diacritic (e.g., -ve, -ce, -ge). It is a serious pedagogical mistake to fail to call to the students' attention the fact that the vowel spelling of "dice" is exactly like that of "die" and the like.

The Spelling of Polysyllables

Our discussion of vowel spelling so far has included only monosyllables; the rules for spelling polysyllables are much more complicated. This state of affairs is accounted for by the fact that polysyllables normally contain only one strongly stressed syllable. They may contain other syllables with reduced or weak stress. Reduction of stress results in changes of vowel quality, so that in most dialects of English only a few vowels occur in weakly stressed syllables: /ə/, /i/, and in some dialects /ɨ/. But most polysyllables are made up of more than one morpheme, and in English a given morpheme tends to retain the same or nearly the same spelling regardless of changes in its sound. For many morphemes, in fact, it is reasonable to speak of a basic pronunciation, usually corresponding quite well to ordinary spelling rules, and various *derived* pronunciations, retaining the same spelling but undergoing sound change. For example, the word "reform," contains two morphemes "re-" and "form," both spelled regularly. The word "reformation" retains their basic spelling, although on the basis of phonetics we would expect the *f* to be doubled after the short vowel /e/, and /ər/ to be spelled *er*, the more frequent spelling. The stem-forming suffix "-a-" is strongly stressed here, indicating its spelling. But in "reformatory" it is weakly stressed, and its spelling is unpredictable from its sound. It is clear that the spelling of polysyllables requires more than the sound of the words themselves; it requires recognition of the morphemes that make up the word and knowledge of how these morphemes are spelled under their strongest stress.

The principle that morphemes tend to be spelled consistently explains the spelling of such words as "slapped" and "hummed": since the morpheme "-ed" retains its basic spelling, the consonants *p* and *m* occur between vowels, where, according to their regular rule, they must be doubled if the preceding vowel is short (as the consonant table shows) despite the fact that phonetically the words end with the consonant clusters /pt/ and /md/.

The rule that morphemes do not change their spelling applies quite generally except in two important instances. In words ending with so-called "silent" *e*, in which the *e* is part of the representation of a long vowel, the *e* is dropped before suffixes beginning with a vowel. The *e* would, of course, be redundant, given the rule that when a single consonant and a vowel follow a vowel, the vowel is long. Notice that when the *e* is part of the consonant graph (as it is in the case of *ce* and *ge*) it can only be dropped if a front vowel (*e*, *i*, or *y*) follows. The other instance is the doubling of the final consonants *p*, *b*, *t*, *d*, *g*, *m*, *n*, and *r* after short vowels when a suffix beginning with a vowel is added. This, of course, is in exact conformity to the rule that short vowels occur before final consonants or consonant groups, not single consonants followed by vowels.

The morphemic structure of words is related to spelling in other ways than its effect on the spelling of vowels. This is particularly obvious in such spellings as *ture* and *cher* for /čər/; *shun*, *tion*, and *sion* for /šən/; and the like. In the case of *ture* and *cher*, it is only necessary to point out that *cher* never occurs in English except as the combination of a base ending in *ch* + the suffix *er* as in "teacher." Similarly, *shun* never occurs as a suffix. Most complex words in English have bases spelled only one way: compare "project," "pro-

jection," "conjecture." Others have two spellings, as in "permit" and
"permission." A few have three. We choose the base according to the suffix:
for example, we use "-mit-" with "-ed," "-ing," and "-s." With "-ive" and
"-ion" we use "-mis-." Thus we say "permits," "permitting," but "permissive"
and "permission." Since the form of the base with "-ive" can be determined
by its pronunciation, and since the form with "-ion" is always the same as
that for "-ive," the simplest solution to such unphonemic spellings as "permission," "derision," "position" is to find the form used with "-ive," then
add "-ion."

It would be inaccurate to give the impression that all polysyllables are
polymorphemic. Some are not, and when they contain weakly stressed
syllables it is often difficult to predict how they will be spelled. A set of words
such as "happen," "bobbin," "button," and "organ" demonstrates this
fact. The sequence /ən/ happens to be the most troublesome of the common
unstressed syllables, but all of them show some degree of irregularity. To
mention only a few, /əl/ is usually spelled *le* but sometimes *el*; /ər/ is usually
er, sometimes *or*, and occasionally even *ar*; /ət/ may be spelled *it*, *ot*, or *et*;
/əd/ is usually *ed* but may be *id*. The examples given thus far are spellings
of final unstressed vowels. The vowels of initial unstressed syllables are easier
to master primarily because they are usually forms of familiar prefixes such
as "ad-" and its variants "as-," "al-," "ap-," "at-," etc., and "in-" and its
variants "il-," "im-," and "ir-." But it is certainly one of the real defects of
the English spelling system that it provides no character to represent the
unstressed vowel, particularly when the vowel occurs in a syllable which is
not a familiar base or affix. There is no alternative to memorizing the
spelling of the unstressed vowels which cannot be determined by word analysis.

"Phonics" and Reading

Spelling is converting spoken words to written ones; reading
is the converse of this. The reader looks at the relations between sounds and
letters from a point of view entirely different from that of the speller. The
good speller acquires the habit of doubling most consonants after short
vowels; the good reader, on the other hand, is conscious of double consonants as a signal that a preceding vowel is short. The reader's task is in
one way more difficult: he must at the same time divide words into their
graphic units (letters and letter combinations like *th*, *ge*, etc.), he must recognize the diacritics (singleness or doubleness of consonants, presence or absence of "silent" *e*, and the like), and he must associate this information
with English phonemes, morphemes, and words. But in another way the
reader's task is easier: the number of alternative pronunciations of a given
graphic unit can almost never be more than two or three, while the same

sound—especially an unstressed vowel—might be spelled half a dozen different ways. Consonants cause almost no difficulty for the reader except the following:

1. *c*, which must be read as /s/ before *e, i, y*; /k/ otherwise.

2. *g* initially, which represents /g/ before back vowels and consonants, /g/ or /ǰ/ otherwise.

3. *se*, read as either /z/ or /s/, as in "please" and "grease." /z/ is by far the most frequent reading.

4. *th*, which initially and medially can represent either /θ/ or /ð/. This graph represents /ð/ initially only in a short list of function words. There are very few instances of medial /θ/ except in technical words from Greek sources.

5. *si*, which represents either /š/ or /ž/, as in "mission," and "confusion." In most instances, *si* represents /š/ after *s*, /ž/ otherwise.

Inferring vowel sounds from letters is far more difficult than inferring consonant sounds. The principal reasons for this state of affairs are the following: English has developed a large and complex vowel-sound system but has limited itself to the five vowel letters borrowed from Latin. In addition, English has tended to keep the foreign spellings of borrowed words, while assigning them an English pronunciation. English has further undergone a number of sound changes without corresponding spelling changes: for example, the sound once represented by "ae" [æː] merged with two different sounds, [e] and [iy]. Thus we have "read" (present) and "read" (past), "lead" (verb) and "lead" (noun), not to mention "bread," "beans," "meadows," "leaves," and many more. Furthermore, dialect variation in English has shown up most strongly in vowel pronunciation, but our standard spelling reflects early modern London dialect with only slight admixture from neighboring dialects. Thus we have "b*ui*ld" from Kentish along with the more usual London "f*i*ll." In reading as in spelling, however, there are some almost wholly predictable sound-letter correspondencs, and there are "best guesses" in every instance. Chart III shows the principal conditioning factors relating to the pronunciation of vowels and the most predictable sound-letter correspondences. It is clear from the chart that the pronunciation of the vowels in the vast majority of monosyllables can be inferred from the spelling by making use of a few simple principles:

1. Vowels before final consonants, doubled consonants, and consonant clusters are "short"; i.e., they represent one of the seven undiphthongized vowel sounds.

2. Vowels in vowel sequences or before single consonants followed by vowel letters are "long"; i.e., they represent one of the complex vowel nuclei.

3. The consonants *r*, *l*, and *w* along with the usually "silent" graph *gh* account for the vast majority of pronunciation variants. These variants are almost always regular.

CHART III. PHONEMES REPRESENTED BY THE ENGLISH
VOWEL LETTERS BASED ON THE THORNDIKE WORD LIST
OF 3000 MONOSYLLABLES

Vowel Letter	Before C or CC	Before Ce or CV	Before rC or r	Before lC	After w	Final	In Vowel Sequences	Common Exceptions
a	/æ/	/ey/	/a/ w-/ɔ/	/a,ɔ/¹	/a,ɔ/¹	/a/	-i,y /ey/ -u,w /ɔ/	said, plaid a, was
e	/e/	/iy/	/ə/	/e/	/e/	/iy/	-i,y /ey/,/iy/ -e /iy/ -a {/iy/ /e/} -u,w {/uw/ /yuw/}	 been heart, learn great, steak, break sew there, where, were
i	/i/	/ay/	/ə/	/i/	/i/		-e {/iy/ /ay/}	find, mind, wild, child, sigh, thigh, high, sight, night, I, ski
o	/a/² /ɔ/	/ow/	/ə/ w-/ə/	/ow/	/ə/-r	/ow/ /uw/(3)	-i,y /oy/ -e /ow/ -a /ow/ -o /uw/ -ok /u/ -u,w /ow/ -u,w /aw/ -ugh {/ə/(3) /ow/(2) /aw/(2) /uw/(2)}	shoe, does, broad great, break foot, blood ought, you come, some, etc. dove, love, etc. none, won, etc. could, would, etc. one
u	/ə/	/uw/	/ə/	/ə/				build, guide, guy, buy put, push, suit
		/yuw/³		/u/p-, b-,f-,m-			-e {/uw/ /yuw/}	guard guest

The most frequent pronunciations are listed *without* numerals.
C stands for consonant or consonant cluster.
¹ Some dialects have only /ɔ/ before *l*, some have only /a/, and some have a mixture of both /ɔ/ and /a/. Usage after *w* is similarly mixed.
² *o* before consonants represents /a/ or /ɔ/ or a mixture of both depending on dialect.
³ All dialects have /yuw/ after consonants other than the alveolars and palatals. After the alveolars and palatals, however, there is considerable dialect variation, and some dialects have only /uw/ in this position.

Learning to recognize spoken monosyllables on the printed page should thus be relatively easy, provided the teaching materials are arranged to allow the most efficient mastery of the rules.

But not all words are monosyllables, and polysyllables present some of the same difficulties for the reader that they present for the speller. The

principle that morphemes retain their basic spelling regardless of changes
in pronunciation is undoubtedly the cause of most of these difficulties. An
obvious example is the preservation of the spelling *ed* for the past tense
morpheme (except in the irregular verbs). This morpheme is pronounced
/t/, /d/, or /əd/ according to whether the preceding phoneme is voiceless,
voiced, or is /t/ or /d/, as in "stopped," "rubbed," and "planted." Fortunately
for the learner, the morphophonemic variation of the past tense morpheme
is something he masters well before coming to school, and once he learns to
respond to *ed* as a morpheme rather than a letter sequence, he has no difficulty with it. The same principle applies to the morphemes for the singular
present tense of verbs and the plural of most nouns. These morphemes are
spelled alike—*es* after final *s*, *sh*, *ch*, or *z*; *s* otherwise. The same pronunciation
variations apply to the noun possessive suffix. Again, the student must learn
to recognize the morpheme and follow the morphophonemic rule to infer
the correct pronunciation. Thus a high degree of competence in word
analysis is essential to successful reading. The kind of analysis involved in
reading includes recognizing familiar bases, prefixes, and suffixes, and
knowing both which are typically stressed and which are unstressed, and
how stress shifts when prefixes and suffixes are added. (For example, when
"-ation" with stressed *a* is added to a word, the base word stress shifts to the
second syllable before the suffix and becomes secondary: cf. "reformation,"
"inoculation," "perturbation," etc.)

A good reader must also be aware of the syllabic structure of words.
That is, he must recognize that words divide into segments characterized
by differing degrees of stress, sometimes with sharply defined boundaries,
sometimes with no clear boundaries at all. Most of the rules for syllable division commonly given out in the schools are nothing more than guides to the
use of the hyphen; they have no relevance to either rules for spelling or rules
for pronunciation. For example, there is said to be a syllable boundary
between double consonants, despite the fact that only one vowel is pronounced and the doubling is merely a vowel diacritic. Similarly the rather
elaborate rules for dividing consonant clusters are in fact only a restatement
of the pronunciation rules for vowels. For example, "reclaim" divides
between "re-" and "-claim" because the vowel /iy/ must occur in an open
syllable but "reclamation" divides between "rec-" and "-lamation" because
a short vowel must be followed by a consonant. But in both words "cl"
represents exactly the same phonetic consonant cluster. The syllable division
rules do, however, contain these valuable insights: some consonant groups
are initial; that is, they occur only at beginnings of words or syllables.
Examples include all the combinations of consonants plus *l* or *r*; *s* followed
by nasals (*sm*, *sn*) or by stops plus nasals; and a few others. Other clusters
are final; they occur only at the ends of words and syllables. Such clusters
include consonants followed by *th*, *d*, or *s* as well as *l* and *r* followed by nasals.
A good reader can use this information to find the points where new stress

levels begin as well as to associate vowels with the appropriate consonants. The old technique of "sounding out" words one letter at a time, usually after spelling the word aloud, proved such a tedious and uncertain way to learn to read that it discredited the whole "phonics" approach to reading. The chances of identifying correctly a word whose sounds are said to be /rə/ /iy/ /fə/ /lə/ /e/ /kə/ /tə/ (= "reflect") are slim. The reader clearly needs to recognize that the initial *r* forms a syllable with the following vowel and is not separable by /ə/, and that *ct* is a similar final cluster. Thus drill in analyzing words into pronounceable units (i.e., syllables) appears to have structural justification.

In summary, we have shown that the English spelling system has an underlying regularity. This regularity is in the form of rules relating spelling to phonology and to grammar. The following general rules seem to operate:

1. English consonant sounds have generally predictable spellings. For example, in such homophonous suffixes as -el and -al, -ous and -ess, the consonant spellings can be predicted from the pronunciation. The vowels must, of course, be identified on the basis of grammatical information.

2. English vowel spellings are predictable (but less so than consonants) in stressed monosyllabic words and in the stressed syllables of polysyllables.

3. In polysyllables vowels whose stress has shifted from strong to weak are spelled as though their stress was strong. Cf. "reform" and "reformation."

4. Affixes often have arbitrary spellings. Cf. "shun" and "-tion," "friend*less*" and "marvel*ous*."

Because of the fact that English spelling is in general related to larger rules of English structure which the child already masters (e.g., phonological and grammatical rules), spelling and reading can be taught most efficiently by relating orthographical rules to the rules the child already knows.

Topics for Investigation

1. What is the probable meaning of the common remark "English is not a phonetic language?" Does this remark involve the assumption that if a language is "phonetic" there is a one-to-one correspondence between its sounds and letters? That its spelling can be inferred from its sounds? Or only that its sounds can be inferred from its spelling?

2. Look up the origins of the spellings of "debt" and "doubt," "island," "diaphragm," and "psychology." What notion (or notions) about the purpose of a writing system do these spellings imply?

3. Should the *l* be pronounced in "calm," "balk," "psalm," etc.? How do you decide? What is the history of the pronunciation of this consonant?

4. Compare your pronunciation of these words with that of other members of your class: "god," "on," "off," "hot," "log," "foggy," "dawn," "don," "bawdy," "body." What differences do you find? To what extent can they be accounted for by differences in regional background? How do these differences relate to the preparation of reading and spelling materials?

5. Observe your pronunciation of the vowel in these words: "smash," "bath," "grass," "laugh," "man." Is the /æ/ diphthongized in any of them? What regional background does diphthongization suggest?

6. Do the same thing with the words "roof," "hoof," "room," "broom," and "spoon."

7. Make a random sampling of the words beginning with *k* in a collegiate dictionary and tabulate them according to whether they are of Old English or some other origin. What can you say about the source of most initial k's in English? At what historical period did most of them enter the English language?

8. Make a list of "spelling demons." To what extent do the words you have listed follow the spelling rules of English—i.e., to what extent is the spelling of each unpredictable? What implications does your answer have for the teaching of reading and spelling?

9. What facts not dealt with in this chapter account for the lack of doubling of consonants after short vowels in such words as "canary," "negation," "basilica," and "about"? How widespread is this phenomenon in English?

10. Make a list of homophones like "metal" and "mettle," or of near homophones like "robin" and "bobbin." In each pair, at least one member will be spelled irregularly. Do you find any way to account for these irregularities? How would you go about teaching them?

11. Test the rule which says that "when two vowels go walking, the first one does the talking" by filling in the chart below with the phonemic symbol which the combined vowel letters represent. The vowel at the left represents the first member of the sequence. The first space is filled. Put parentheses around very unusual letter combinations or pronunciations.

	a	*e*	*i,y*	*o*	*u,w*
a	—				
e	*iy(ey)(e)*				
i					
o					
u					

Suggestions for Further Reading

The analysis of the English sound system presented in this chapter is essentially the one developed by George L. Trager and Henry Lee Smith in *An Outline of English Structure*, first published in 1951 and reprinted by the American Council of Learned Societies in 1963. It has been used with some modifications by W. Nelson Francis in *The Structure of American English* (New York: The Ronald Press Company, 1958), and in a number of other general studies of modern English structure. Although the phonemic symbols are different, this is also essentially the analysis used in the *Roberts English Series* (New York: Harcourt, Brace & World, Inc., 1966).

Some excellent studies of regional variation in English sound systems include the following: Raven I. McDavid, Jr., "American English Dialects" (in Francis, 1958, pp. 480–543); Hans Kurath and Raven I. McDavid, Jr., *The Pronunciation of English in the Atlantic States* (Ann Arbor: University of Michigan, 1961); Thomas H. Wetmore, "The Low-central and Low-back Vowels in the English of the Eastern United States," *Publication of the American Dialect Society*, XXXII (1959).

Social dialect variation also affects sound systems and, in turn, the basis for the preparation of reading and spelling materials. Two important studies of this subject are Roger Shuy, ed., *Social Dialects and Language Learning* (Champaign, Ill.: National Council of Teachers of English, 1965), and William Labov, *The Social Stratification of English in New York City* (Washington, D.C.: Center for Applied Linguistics, 1966).

A recent, extensive study of sound-letter correspondence in English is U.S.O.E. Cooperative Research Report No. 3090, *A Study of Selected Spelling-to-Sound Correspondence Patterns* (1966), by Richard L. Venezky and Ruth H. Weir.

Sounds and Letters
in School Materials

If our writing system corresponds to our spelling system in any general way (and our discussion above has shown that it does), then learning to read and spell can be done most efficiently if the general principles relating sounds and letters are made use of. But the use of phonics rules in reading and graphic rules in spelling has fallen into serious disrepute. This must be true either because the rules have been inaccurate or because they have been presented in the wrong way or both. "Both" is probably the correct answer; the confusion of meanings of words like "diphthong," "short" and "long" vowel, "blend," and the like in school materials could only lead to misunderstandings, as does the widespread custom of talking about sounds in terms of their spelling. It is equally obvious that memorizing the information on Charts I and II in Chapter VII would almost certainly be unrewarding. We should consider first what the characteristics of good spellers and readers may be and how the use of phonic-graphic information may be best applied in developing these characteristics.

A good speller must know how to spell correctly the words he commonly uses. Besides this, however, he must also know how to spell the common *morphemes*, including prefixes, suffixes, and bases. He should know how to spell such forms as *ceive* (as in "receive," "perceive," etc.), *tain* (as in "pertain," "retain,"), *sion, tion, ize,* and numerous other common word parts. But, most important, he should know how to spell almost infallibly words he does not commonly use—new words and even nonsense words. Although a child may have memorized all the randomly assorted words in his school spelling book (if it is a typical one) he is still a bad speller if he cannot spell accurately a new word like "mipe" or "pule" or "reff." Similarly, no matter how many words he may have memorized, if, when he is asked to spell a word he can pronounce and has seen in print, his spelling does not represent at least the phonetic shape of the word, he still has a long way to go. The child who spells a word like "music" *miscu* has a serious spelling problem; the one who spells it *muzick* is well on his way to becoming a good speller.

The good speller knows the possible spelling variants of a given phoneme and he knows which to choose under given circumstances. We need to consider in detail what this knowledge involves and how it may be obtained.

The good speller must know in the first place what spelling is—that is, that spelling is finding a written representation for spoken words. Unhappily, most school materials suggest the exact opposite of this principle by their use of random word lists, by their disordered rules (if they give any at all), and by their failure to distinguish deviant from normal spellings and to lead the child to mastery of the latter before bringing up the special problems of the former.

In addition, the good speller must have a strong awareness of sounds as segments—he must recognize that, say, "bill," "till," "pill," "kill," "dill," and "gill" end alike but have different beginning sounds. Furthermore, he needs to know that the beginning sounds of these words are the same as the final sounds of "tab," "tat," "tap," "tack," "tad," and "tag." He must be conscious of the fact that all words are made up of a very few different sound segments. There are a number of ways to help children obtain this consciousness: through having them make up minimal-pair series like the ones just mentioned, through such familiar activities as making up rhymes or saying tongue twisters and through making up or modifying phrases using vowel harmony, such as "black hat," "red hen," "chicken licken" (not to mention "Batman" and "Crabby Appleton").

A second thing the good speller is conscious of is sequence—that is, that sounds follow each other in time and that this order in time corresponds to the left-right order on the printed page. Difficulties with letter sequence are common among beginning spellers, and the teacher should provide activities which develop this awareness. Any sort of word-building activity will lead to a consciousness of sequence—adding consonants to words that end with vowels such as "by," "tie," "high," "fry," "fly," etc. (all of which can be followed by /t/); "day," "hay," "may," "ray," etc., which can be followed by /l/, and the like. Adding consonants at the beginning allows all sorts of possibilities: seeing how many new words can be made up by adding /s/—"spill," "skill," "still," "school," "spool," etc. Putting /s/ before stops, nasals, and /l/; putting stops and fricatives before /r/, /l/, /w/, and /y/; and adding nasals and the suffixes /θ/, /t/, /d/, /s/, and /z/ at the ends of words will lead to an awareness of sequence. So will reversing the order of the sounds in words, which, like word-building, may have an element of surprise: "tap" becomes "pat," "eat" becomes "tea," and so on. An ingenious teacher can readily turn any of these activities into games. (It should be emphasized that in the early stages of sequence training, the emphasis must be on the order in which the sound features occur. The children have to be aware of sounds as occurring first, second, third, etc., before left-right sequence in writing can mean anything to them.)

Awareness of the syllabic structure of words is also one of the skills of the competent speller. He does not need to know syllable boundaries—he can struggle with the hyphen (which is useful only if one needs to break words at margins anyway) when he is in junior high or high school. But he does need to be aware of the rhythm of stress increase and decrease in English words and phrases, since he will spell more successfully if his basic unit is larger than the letter but not so large as most polysyllabic words. In "sounding out" a word in preparation for spelling it, dealing with one syllable at a time is better than trying to deal with one sound unit at a time, particularly since most vowels and consonants cannot be uttered in isolation without serious distortion. Awareness of stress and, along with it, of the syllable can be taught with any of the familiar rhythmic children's songs and games. Counting the beats, gesturing to show increase and decrease of stress, letting the children make up last lines for rimes or limericks will all lead to a consciousness of the syllable.

It goes without saying that successful spellers are highly sensitive to the shapes of letters and to the features that distinguish one from another. The child who has a vague awareness of the general shape of words may do well enough with words like "lay" or "yet" but he will almost certainly have trouble with words like "manner" or "flight." This is an awareness that is even more important in reading, and it will be discussed in more detail below.

Should beginning spellers learn the alphabet in the traditional order? They will have to learn it at some time, since it is our most common way of putting words and names in order. But the order of the letters of the alphabet suggests nothing at all about the rules that govern their use or the sounds they correspond to. A beginning speller certainly needs to know letter names—it is much too difficult to try to describe spellings without them—but there is something to be said for dealing with the letters in other than alphabetical order. For example, it is important to know the vowel letters as a group, and it is almost equally important to recognize as a group the stops, the fricatives, the nasals, and the oral continuants. As for the letter names themselves, the teacher may find that made-up names approximating the sounds the letters stand for may be more helpful. Some letter names are obviously misleading: *h*, *w*, *c*, and *y* are certainly badly named. And for most letters it is not necessary to add the /iy/ vowel which our traditional alphabet requires.

Once the child has a grasp of the way English spelling works, he is ready to deal with the central task involved in learning to spell: learning the sound-letter correspondences. Some spellers learn this skill despite bad classroom materials, but it is clear that spelling can be taught more efficiently than it usually is. Since the child is expected to master rules, his lesson materials must be chosen so that the focus is on similarities in the structure of words. A random or subject-matter oriented approach to spelling word selection can only delay the child's mastery of English spelling rules. Furthermore, the rules must be presented in a particular order, with the most pervasive regularities presented first and the more exceptional ones later. And the words should be chosen so that no rules still undiscovered are presupposed. The rules should, in general, be presented in this order: one rule at a time, most pervasive rules first, new rules dependent only on rules already taught. Assuming these basic principles, spelling word lists should be composed in the following way: The first words taught should be monosyllables. They should be composed of two elements: a pivot and a variable. The pivots should be word parts like *-at* or *ba-*. Only the most regular of the short vowels (*i, e, a, u*) should be used in the pivots. The variables should be drilled thoroughly both initially and finally. In addition, the digraphs *th* (representing /θ/) and *sh, w,* and *h* may be introduced at this stage. *Sh* and *th* should be taught as unitary characters. The children will soon discover that *w, y,* and *h* occur only at the beginnings of the words they make up. It is taken for granted that at this stage the children will not be burdened with words like "consonant" and "vowel" and that, above all, they will not be told such things as that "these consonants that do not double after a short vowel are the most important ones." The whole purpose of an ordered, adequately drilled presentation is that the child should not need to learn rules as rules, but rather that he should acquire them as habits—that he learn to spell, say, final /p/ as *p*, not *pp*, automatically—without reference to a formal rule.

At this stage (in order to make it easier for the children to compose sentences) the teacher may wish to introduce a small set of words whose spelling must be memorized. Such words might include "a," "the," and "can." But extended, subject-matter related lists should be avoided entirely. Sets of pictures with spaces for writing names would be far better: a pan, a rat, a man, a bat, etc. The children will enjoy making up words on the word parts they already know, and they may get an even greater thrill from combining them into sentences, particularly comic ones such as "The man bit a rat"—perhaps drawing their own illustrations. Suppose the children come up with words like "nat" for "gnat": should they be corrected? In my view, they should not. It would be disastrous for them to begin at this early stage to develop the inhibitions and terrors which make writing so painful for most high school and college students. Whatever they produce should be accepted so long as it conforms to the rules already taught. If not, they should have further drill. The drill, by the way, should take the form of choral responses, taking turns making up words, and the like, not the old-fashioned but still occasionally heard *b, a, t* "bat," *c, a, t* "cat" refrain.

The next consonants to be taught should be the regular doubling ones: *f, l,* and (since we are dealing only with monosyllables containing short vowels) *s, z, k, ch,* and *j*. The last three will require considerable drill because they add another, different consonant instead of simply doubling. Like *th* and *sh*, the graph *ch* should be taught as a unitary consonant; the students should learn that *tch* is double *ch*, that *ck* is double *k*, and that *dge* is double *j*. They will not need to be told this, of course, if they are permitted to infer it correctly from selected examples.

The long vowels can best be introduced by using them first at the ends of words. Final *ee, oo, ow* = /ow/, *oe*, and *ie* should be taught first. The children will easily make up new words by adding consonants to the first three. With the last two it should be fairly easy for them to make the adjustment to putting the consonant between the two letters of the vowel digraph; thus "tie" becomes "tile," "lie" becomes "life," "pie" becomes "pipe," "hoe" becomes "hope," "doe" becomes "dome," and the like. Once the children have mastered the rule that *e* can be separated by a consonant from the vowel it forms part of, they should be introduced to the rest of the "silent e" forms: *a-e, u-e*, and *e-e*. If the children are being allowed to make up their own spelling lists, they will be now be coming up with a great many incorrectly spelled words, since the long vowels permit more variation than do the short ones. Instead of correcting the children, the teacher's best tactic at this point may be to simply "save" the incorrect words and focus the lessons on the correct ones. The long vowel alternatives must be presented anyway. Perhaps the best start is to show how *y* occurs at the ends of words. The class can begin by making up words with a final digraph like *-ay*. When they have a good list, hopefully containing "lay," "pay," "may," "ray," and the like, they can be told to add consonants. The teacher then shows them how *ay* becomes *ai* within a word. There are very few words containing /oy/ in English, but the spelling of this diphthong should probably be brought up at this point. The children can find a few pairs of the type "boy"—"boil," "toy"—"toil," and the like. They should then be ready for the two remaining digraphs, *ea* and *oa*. They will have already discovered that long vowels may be spelled in more ways than one: they now know *ow* and *o-e* for /ow/, *ai* (*y*) and *a-e* for /ey/, and *ee* and *e-e* for /iy/. *Ea* and *oa* give them a third way to write the complex nuclei /iy/ and /ow/. There is little to be gained by trying to explain why one spelling is used and not another; the only satisfactory way for children to learn to distinguish "load" and "lode," "seam" and "seem" is for them to associate each word having a particular spelling with the other words spelled in the same way. They should be given enough practice with, for example, the *ea* words by themselves so that they have little trouble remembering which words with the vowel /iy/ belong to that set.

We have not mentioned several vowels that do not seem to fit particularly well at any point in this program. They include /aw/, /ɔ/, /u/, and /uw/. It is possible that the vowel /aw/, spelled *ou* or *ow*, fits best in the lessons that deal with the alternation of medial and final letters. We have also not mentioned /ɔ/, written *o, a, ou*, and *aw*. This vowel varies greatly from dialect to dialect. In dialects which do not distinguish /a/ and /ɔ/, such words as "off," "on," and "log" can be included along with the short vowels. In other dialects a series of lessons may have to be devoted to this vowel, not all at once but one spelling at a time. The same thing must be said for the spelling *oo*, which represents both /u/ and /uw/. In most dialects there are very few words (but some extremely common ones) in which *oo* stands for /u/; in others, however, there are a great many. We have also not mentioned such unusual spellings as *ei* for /iy/, *io* for /yə/, and the like. Most of these spellings occur in words of foreign origin, and they should probably be taught along with word analysis rather than as part of the spelling program for basic phonetic rules.

Once monosyllables are mastered, the children should be ready for disyllables. They need to learn first that the principle of consonant doubling, which applies to graphs like *f*, *s*, etc., must now be extended to nearly all of the consonants. The doubled forms they have learned for *ch*, *j*, and *k* they can now apply medially after short vowels as well as finally. They will have no new doubled forms to learn if the monosyllables have been mastered —only the principle that the nondoubling consonants double in disyllables. The disyllables, of course, introduce the problem of the unstressed vowel. It is clear that this problem, like the *ea*, *ee*, *e-e* problem, can best be handled by using lists of words with the same spelling. For example, such words as "ribbon," "button," "common," should be taught together, as should "fountain," "curtain," "bargain," and "certain." Sometimes the children will be able to associate a meaning with the unstressed syllable, as they should be able to do with *-en* in "taken," "eaten," "given," and "ridden." This serves both as a key to the spelling and as an introduction to the structure of complex words, which should constitute the major part of their study from this point on.

The simplest way to approach the analysis of words is by combining bases and affixes which do not involve spelling change. Suffixes like "-ly" and "-ness" can be added to monosyllabic adjectives, "re-" to monosyllabic verbs, and "-ish" to monosyllabic nouns. Once the principle is well understood, the children can begin to expand polysyllables. A good beginning is with disyllables ending in *y*, in which they can use again a rule they have already learned—that *y* occurs at the ends of words, *i* within them. Thus "ready" becomes "readi-" before "-ness," "happy" becomes "happi-" before "-ly" and the like. A second widespread rule which relates to what they have already learned is the rule that so-called silent *e* is dropped before suffixes beginning with a vowel but not otherwise, as in "hoping" and "hopeful." They already know that a vowel before a consonant cluster is short, which explains why the *e* must be retained before consonants. They also know that when a single consonant occurs between vowels, the first vowel is long, which explains why the *e* is not needed before suffixes beginning with vowels. The majority of complex words in English involve borrowed affixes, often with special effects on pronunciation and spelling which will not have been covered in the study of monosyllables and disyllables with common affixes. It is essential that these words be taught as sets involving the application of the same processes; the attempt to learn by rote all the complex words of English is far too big a task to be undertaken if there is a systematic and logical way to go about achieving the same goal. For example, the *ceive* words, which involve a spelling change in the base and a stress shift are relatively easy to master if it is clear that not randomly different spellings but recurrences of the same processes are involved. Thus the shifts involved in going from, say, "receive" to "receivable," "reception," apply in exactly the same way to "deceive," "perceive," and "conceive." Similarly with the numerous *mit* words, such as "permit," "commit," "remit," "submit," which have a base form to which tense suffixes are added (-ed, -ing, -s) and a modified form for conversions to other classes: a nominalized -*mission*, adjectival -*missible*, and, of course, the adverbial, number, and comparative suffixes which may be added to these. A student who is aware of the spelling of English prefixes and suffixes and who knows bases as members of sets with similar variations will be able to spell the vast majority of English polysyllables. There will still be a residue that must be memorized—words like "diaphragm" and "phalanx." But the student who has been taken step by step from the most basic to the most complex rules of English spelling is equipped to deal with spelling intelligently. He will have to master some parts of some new words through brute memory, but the vast majority of the new spellings he encounters will reflect processes with which he is thoroughly familiar.

The teaching of reading has been so widely discussed and is still so controversial that one approaches it with considerable hesitation. Yet, as has been noted before, it is not a branch of ethics or theology: facts are available to demonstrate whether, as the "whole word" advocates suggest, English spelling is too irregular to submit to a phonics approach or not. Our observations thus far suggest that there is a high degree of regularity in the relation between sounds and letters—not as much as there should be, as experiments with the Pitman *i.t.a.* approach seem to show, but far more so than most ordinary reading materials suggest. The good reader is the reader who can find quickly and accurately *language* on the printed page. That is, he finds phonemes, morphemes, words, phrases, sentences, and larger units represented there. He must be able to respond to print just as he would respond to the same language units in conversation—he will understand more or less well, get the direct meaning of the utterance or not, find implications or miss them—but he will recognize the utterance as language. He will know what the words are and how they relate to each other. His degree of understanding should be no less than for the same utterance heard in conversation. Thus the more directly the beginning reader can relate what he is learning to what he already knows, the more rapidly he can progress. The beginning reader needs an awareness of words as consisting of segments, the ability to identify sound segments as the same or different, awareness of sequence in the phonemic structure of words, the ability to distinguish letters, awareness of the rules that relate letters to sounds, and an understanding of the makeup of complex words—the ability to divide words into syllables and to identify the same affixes and bases even in different words. All of these skills have been discussed in connection with spelling, and suggestions have been made for teaching them. Two of these abilities are of such basic importance to reading, however, that they deserve further comment: the ability to distinguish letter shapes and the ability to recognize the syllabic structure of words.

The letter-shapes problem is a serious one because from the beginning the student encounters one of the frustrating facts about the English writing system—that the same grapheme (or set of representations of the same written unit) has several different shapes, some quite unlike the others. Most capital letters, for example, bear no resemblance to their lower-case variants, and type faces very from script to block letter to roman to italic to text. It is obvious that the simplest and clearest type face should be used consistently for beginning readers—either block letter (which so-called manuscript handwriting imitates) or roman. The use of only lower-case letters in the *i.t.a.* system is on the right track, although capitals would certainly have been the better choice. A little observation shows that both the capital and lower-case letters of English fall into sets distinguished by simple rearrangements of parts. For example, all English capital letters except *Q* are made of the following parts: |, —, ¯, /, \, (, and). These parts can occur simultaneously or in sequence. They divide into sets according to their degree of similarity: *P*, *B*, and *R* are different from each other by a single feature, as are *R* and *K*, *C* and *G*, *M* and *N*, *O* and *Q*, *E* and *F*, *V* and *W*, *X* and *Y*, *L* and *I*. It is these minimally different features which will cause the beginner the most difficulty and which should be taught in special lessons focusing on the distinctive graphic features. The lower case letters are much less systematic than the capitals. They do include some minimally different sets: *b*, *d*, *p*, and *g*; *m* and *n*; *f* and *t*; *i* and *j*; *v* and *w*; *n* and *h*; *c* and *o*; *n* and *u*; *q* and *g*. Drills with minimal pairs, like those used to teach distinctive phonological features, appear to be the only way to provide clearly focused teaching of these graphic differences. It is easy to find phrases which serve this purpose: "a bat," "a rat"; "batting" and "patting"; "a ring" and "a king," etc. As in all teaching, the best teaching of the letter shapes is teaching that spares the child as much brute memorization as possible and which allows him to make use of the underlying system, to the extent that the English graphic system has one.

A thorough grasp of the syllabic structure of English words is even more essential for reading than it is for spelling. Because the consonants of English do not occur in isolation, the beginning reader in the process of "sounding out" words must combine them with vowels. But if he combines them with /iy/ or /e/ or /ey/, as their traditional letter names suggest, he will surely have serious difficulty in making a word of the sequence of sounds he has discovered. Beginning lessons in relating the sounds and letters of English cannot contain units smaller than the syllable. First lessons should be monosyllabic and should contain minimal differences of the type mentioned above. Drill with monosyllables should continue at least until the child has mastered all the common consonants with the short vowels. Then he should begin combining these monosyllables into disyllabic words on the pattern of "batman," "rimrock," "tincan," "boxcar," and the like, moving to less familiar initial and final syllables but making maximum use of what is already familiar—"happen," "matching," "batter," "remark"—so that the child develops and maintains the habit of working from syllable units, rather than from letters, in his attempts to find spoken words on the printed page. This ability, as noted above, involves being able to recognize initial and final consonant clusters and to use this information to find the units to "sound out"; and being able to make the shift from one stress level to another when reading aloud. Fortunately, there are so many regular monosyllabic and disyllabic words in English that it is possible to provide at the same time drill in sound-letter relationships and real stories that can hold the children's attention and give them the motivation that comes from knowing that they are really reading. The following story, quoted by permission from the Miami Linguistic Series reader *Hot Corn Muffins*, is an example.

PLANTING THE CORN

Chuck
Chuck is a chipmunk.
Jen
Jen is a hen.
Chub
Chub is a cub.
Jen Hen is digging and digging.
Jen Hen is planting corn.
Jen Hen digs and plants, and digs and plants.
Chuck Chipmunk and Chub Cub are running up the hill.
Chuck Chipmunk is running with a big sack on his back, and Chub Cub is running with a fish net in his hands.
  It is hot, and Chuck and Chub are hot. They stop at Jen Hen's cabin and sit on a rock to rest.
  "It's hot, isn't it, Jen Hen?"
  "Yes, it is hot! and I'm hot!
  "Chuck and Chub, help plant this corn.
  "Help plant this corn so I can rest."
  "No, Jen Hen, I can't help. I can't help plant the corn. I am going on up the hill."
  "I'm going on up the hill to pick a sack of nuts."[1]

---

[1] *Miami Linguistic Readers, Level Six*, Ralph F. Robinett, Production Director (Miami, Florida: D. C. Heath & Company, 1966).

It should be emphasized that what has been developed so far is a program for introductory reading. It provides the basis from which real reading competence can be developed; it is not true that to be a good reader all one has to do is be able to pronounce all the words on a page correctly. Everything that has been said about grammar and that will be said about words is applicable to reading. A good reader must be able to infer grammatical relations from print and he must be able to determine correctly how words are being used—to determine whether, for example, a given occurrence of the word "club" is noun or verb and whether it has meaning features relevant to organizations or warfare or sport. The listener makes inferences of this kind by interpreting contours of stress, pitch, and time; by drawing on his store of information about the structure of complex words; and by inferring from probabilities of occurrence in given contexts what grammatically or semantically ambiguous words and phrases may mean. The listener, in other words, is in the continuous process of forming hypotheses about the language he is receiving, reducing the number of alternatives as he gets more information, drawing on information he has already established to interpret the new signals coming to him. His interpretation of sentences actually involves a certain amount of sentence production—of framing hypothetical sentences to be retained or rejected on the basis of further signals. No child is reading until he is doing much this same sort of thing. Mere word recognition is no more reading than it is listening. The child must make a correct grammatical and semantic analysis of what he is reading as well as a correct phonological one. Thus reading teaching must require from the very beginning the inference of correct intonation patterns (to be read into the text just as they are read into spoken utterances on the basis of function words and word relationships). A phrase such as "in all the little houses" should have a stress pattern approximating weak (ˇ) – secondary (ˆ) – weak – secondary – strong (ˊ). A pattern of strong – strong – strong – strong – strong totally obscures the grammatical relationships within the phrase, and reading teaching which never gets beyond correct word recognition is almost certain to leave the child in this grammarless stage. What this implies about teaching is that advancement in a reading program should be governed by the child's mastery of the ability to get the whole message from a printed sentence, not merely from his ability to identify words. This progress will be indicated by his supplying suitable patterns of intonation. It will also be indicated by his ability to rephrase, either paraphrase or transform, what he has read. It is up to the teacher to supply the model for this kind of reading and to maintain an analytic question-and-answer sequence which will make it clear to the child what he is looking for on the page—not a string of spoken words but the whole linguistic content from morphemes to the complex aspects of style which it is possible to express in English.

Topics for Investigation

1. Obtain a set of spelling papers from a fourth, fifth, or sixth grade class. Which of the following general kinds of errors do you find:

    a. The first letter or letters of a word spelled correctly, the rest a jumble.

    b. The general configuration of the word correct (that is, tall and short letters in about the right places), but the spelling random otherwise.

    c. Errors with affixes of the type "-le" for "-al," "-shun" for "-tion," and the like.

    d. Errors in modifying the base to provide for affixation: e.g., final "e" not dropped, final consonant not doubled, final "y" not changed to "i."

    e. Errors in bases involving incorrect doubling of consonants or the incorrect use of vowel monographs and digraphs.

What kind of lessons would you prescribe for each of these difficulties?

2. Compare five or six elementary spelling textbooks. Which of them have these characteristics:

    a. Careful ordering, so that most pervasive and most basic regularities are presented first.

    b. Explanation (or drills) in terms of the most general application of rules: e.g., the fact that "dropping silent 'e' " and "doubling the final consonant" constitute parts of the same rule based on the general principle that in the string VCCV the first vowel is short but in VCV it is long?

3. What can you say about the following common principles for putting together spelling lessons:

    a. Spelling should be taught by means of word lists given out on Monday and tested on Friday.

    b. Spelling words should be chosen from the child's reading in other subjects, such as social studies.

    c. Spelling words should be related conceptually—e.g., all about a holiday, about an excursion, and the like.

    d. The spelling of a word can be learned best by (1) looking at the word; (2) picturing it mentally; (3) spelling it while looking at it; (4) spelling it while not looking at it; (5) looking at it and repeating the process if necessary.

4. Examine several current lower school reading series. Which of the following characteristics do you find:

a. Careful attention to limiting the number of new sound-letter correspondences introduced in each lesson.

b. Provision of sufficient drill for each such correspondence.

c. Limitation of the number of items in each lesson which must be mastered as whole words (e.g., "of," "might").

d. Attention to the ordering of and provision for practice in recognizing grammatical structures in print.

Is the language like that of the children who will use the series in vocabulary and in sentence type and complexity? If not, what theory of reading seems to account for the differences?

Suggestions for Further Reading

The best discussions of the relevance of linguistics to reading are to be found in Charles C. Fries, *Linguistics and Reading* (New York: Holt, Rinehart & Winston, Inc., 1952) and Carl A. Lefevre, *Linguistics and the Teaching of Reading* (New York: McGraw-Hill Book Company, 1964).

Some important shorter studies include the following: Eleanor J. Gibson, Anne Pick, Harry Osser, and Marcia Hammond, "The Role of Grapheme-Phoneme Correspondence in the Perception of Words," *American Journal of Psychology*, LXXV (1962), 554–70; Part II of Roger Brown's *Words and Things* (Glencoe, Illinois: The Free Press, 1958); and the excellent collection of articles in *New Perspectives in Reading Instruction*, Albert J. Mazurkiewicz, ed. (New York: Pitman Publishing Corporation, 1964).

Words

CHAPTER 9 Grammatical classes and phonological rules by themselves are but abstractions. There are no sentences without words. The error of assuming, as many people seem to do, that learning a language is learning a long list of words, is no more serious than its opposite—assuming that knowing the abstract structure of a language is knowing the language. There is a basic vocabulary without which it is totally impossible to function in English, and there are innumerable specialized vocabularies, often overlapping, some of which every participating member of an English-speaking society must control. In this chapter, we will consider what it means to know words.

Although the word "word" is used habitually, finding a satisfactory definition for it is very difficult. We commonly call "words" those linguistic units that are separated by white space in print. But just as printers' conventions do not correspond very well to the actual sound system of English, our conventional use of white space may not represent anything more than a tradition, with little basis in grammar or phonology. The differences in the practice of dictionaries in using hyphens, space, or no space in so-called compounds suggest that writers of English are not certain what criteria should be used to decide whether a sequence is one word, two words, or something in between. (Compare "all right" and "already"; "into" and "out of.")

The problem is essentially this: is there a unit smaller than the phrase but larger than the morpheme? Another way to put the same question would be to ask whether the morpheme sequence "kindness" is different in some regular way from the sequence "being kind." Their similarities are clear: each consists of parts which can be replaced by other morphemes. "Kindness" can become "happiness" and "being kind" can become "being happy." Furthermore, both can occupy the same position in sentences: "Kindness is a virtue," "Being kind is a virtue." But there are some important differences. First of all, nothing can be inserted between "kind" and "-ness" without totally changing one part of it or the other. "Kindliness" is not a case of adding "-li-" to "kindness"; it is a case of replacing "kind" with "kindly," a different unit altogether. But "being kind" can become "being very

111

kind," "being as kind as possible," and the like without changing either "being" or "kind." "Kindness" is an example of the combination of a free form with a bound form; that is, the relatively more free form "kind" (which can occur in a wide variety of contexts as well as at the beginnings and ends of utterances) is combined with the relatively more bound form "-ness," which never occurs except after units like "kind," units with such other characteristics as coming after "be," as occurring with qualifiers such as "very." "Kindness" is thus different in an important way from phrases such as "being kind." But it is also clearly different from a unitary morpheme, since it consists of two parts, either of which is replaceable without affecting the identity of the other, while morphemes cannot be divided without being reduced to meaninglessness. It seems reasonable to give the name "word" to combinations of free and bound forms, since they are different from phrases on the one hand and morphemes on the other.

But consider such morpheme combinations as "blackboard," "black belt," and "black cow." These are combinations of free forms, and they are in that respect like phrases. If we apply the test of separability, we find that neither "blackboard" nor "black belt" can be separated very freely. "Black cow," however, can be expanded to "black and white cow" or "black dairy cow" without affecting the meaning of the original phrase. Thus there seem to be some combinations of free forms which are like free-bound combinations in being inseparable. "Blackboard" and "black belt" are different from "black cow" in another important respect: they have the kind of stress and time pattern which we associate with disyllabic morphemes or combinations with bound forms, a sequence of primary and tertiary stress (i.e., a level of stress between secondary and weak), while "black cow" seems to have a secondary-primary stress pattern. "Blackboard" and "black belt" also do not have the rather marked slowing which indicates the boundary between "black" and "cow." We can probably distinguish words from smaller or larger units reasonably well by combining the criteria mentioned so far: a word consists of at least one morpheme which may be accompanied by free or bound morphemes or both. It cannot be divided without changing its overall meaning or the meaning of its parts, and it has one of a class of fixed stress and time patterns characterized by containing not more than one strong (primary or secondary) stress and by "close" juncture; that is, by permitting no significant slowing or pause. Most "words" listed in dictionaries and traditionally written with white space boundaries fit this definition. The remaining problems involved compound words which are in the process of becoming unitary words (like "air space") or that are rather limited in freedom of occurrence but still separable (such as "-'s" in "the king's hat" and "the king of England's hat"). They also include the words which are phonologically the same but different in grammatical class or meaning.

A discussion topic at the end of Chapter One mentioned the problem of words like "seem" and "seam," "have" (verb) and "have" (aux), and "to bore" (drill holes) and "to bore" (weary by being dull). The difference in spelling of "seem" and "seam" probably explains why most people would never think of them as the same word, although by the phonological and grammatical criteria we have worked out thus far, they are the same. Differences and similarities in spelling are historical accidents: historically different words may acquire the same pronunciation and spelling, and the same word may split into two given the right combination of dialect separation and mixture. But the two spellings "seem" and "seam" do not occur at random. One always represents a noun, the other a verb. In addition, they have no similarity in meaning; i.e., a translation or definition of one could not possibly apply to the other. The "ea-ee" difference in these words gives reliable grammatical and semantic information, but no phonological information. It is reasonable to regard "seam" and "seem" as separate because their grammatical class membership and meanings are different.

"Have" (verb) and "have" (aux) are different in exactly the same way, despite their similarity in spelling and historical origin. The state of affairs can be put in somewhat this way: (1) There is a class of words such that they occur as head words in VP's, are transitive, do not have a passive transformation; to this class belong "weigh," "resemble," "have," etc. (2) The English auxiliary phrase contains an optional morpheme "have" which requires past-participle suffixation of the following element and is inflected for tense, etc. In summary, we have two nonoverlapping grammatical classes, each of which has a member called "have." If it were the case that "weigh," "resemble," etc. could be used as auxiliaries, or that the other auxiliaries could be used as main verbs, we would probably want to call our two "haves" the same word. But this is not the case. In addition, of course, there is the semantic difference between these two words: the auxiliary has nothing to do with possessing, holding, and getting—the meanings of "have" (verb).

The two "to bores" present quite a different problem. These words are grammatically very similar; they are transitive verbs, they have a passive transformation, they occur with the same auxiliaries. They have the same historical origin and are listed by most dictionaries under a single heading. But there are some grammatical and semantic contexts which they do not have in common: to bore a piece of stone is always taken as meaning to make a hole in a piece of stone, whereas to bore a person and to make a hole in him may be quite different things. While the second meaning of "bore," "to weary," was undoubtedly a metaphorical extension of the first meaning, it no longer is taken as a metaphor. With human-noun objects, "bore" has totally lost its associations with drilling. Compare "his ingratitude stabs me," "her continual chatter grinds on my nerves," and similar still fully metaphorical uses of words. It seems reasonable to call the two "bores" two different words on grounds essentially the same as those we used to distinguish "seam" from "seem": "bore" in the grammatical and semantic context *human noun* is unrelated to the "bore" that occurs with nonhuman nouns. It does not seem reasonable to regard words as the same even if they are spelled alike if they have totally different meanings in different, predictable grammatical and semantic contexts.

With words as with sounds and grammatical classes, there seems to be an inevitable residue that cannot be classified easily. This is true primarily because language is changing constantly; Shakespeare would most likely have said "the king's hat of England"; "-'s" has become more word-like since the seventeenth century. And compounding is such a lively process for word coinage in modern English that it is inevitable that we should sometimes be uncertain whether a given sequence is separable or not, has a fixed stress pattern, or has a unitary meaning. And metaphorical extension is a continuing process leading to the division of unitary words into distinct new words.

The word "word" is hard to define—but no more so than most other words. Words *mean* on different levels and in different ways. We will not attempt a formal theory of definition such as would be appropriate in a study of the philosophy of language but only point out some of the ways in which words can be defined. Perhaps the most obvious kind of definition is pointing: the word "table" is defined as "that over there." Two things are clear about this kind of definition: it can only be applied to names or events or qualities which belong to immediate experience. And it only works infallibly with proper nouns. Pointing will define "John W. Peterson, III," but, as anyone who has taught foreign learners of English has discovered, it will not work with "table"—at least it will not work with only one table. A foreigner watching a native speaker of English point to a table and say "table" might possibly make the right inference, particularly if his language also has a word for tables; but he is just as likely to say to himself, "Aha, *table* means a wooden object" or "*Table* means a piece of furniture" or "*Table* means a brown thing." It would only be after he had associated the word "table" with end tables and coffee tables, dining tables and operating tables, wooden tables, steel tables, brown tables and white tables that he would finally grasp what is meant by the word "table."

There are several key points to be made from this observation: First of all, even the name of an object belonging to our everyday experience is an abstraction. That is, the concept we name "table" is abstracted from our experience of many tables, and is the name for whatever common features they may have—a wide flat, raised surface with no superstructure. Thus the meaning of a word is the whole set of features it is associated with and which distinguish it from all other words. Thus "boy" means "human, male, child." It is distinguished from "girl," which means "human" and "child" but not "male"; from "man," which means "human" and "male," but not "child," and so on. Finally, knowing the meaning of a word means being able to fit it into a total conceptual framework, to know where it fits in the dissection (or categorization) of reality which is made by a given language.

That words can be placed on a "ladder of abstraction" is a familiar notion and one with important implications. It is obvious that the sequence "matter," "animate object," "animal," "vertebrate," "mammal," "primate," "Homo sapiens," "Swede," "boy," "Ed Peterson" illustrates a scale of declining abstractness. Attempting to define each term will show exactly what this means. "Matter" is nothing more than concrete substance. "Animate objects" are living concrete substances. "Animals" are moving, non-photosynthesizing living concrete substances. "Vertebrates" are moving, nonphotosynthesizing, living, concrete substances with backbones. "Mammals" are milk-giving, moving, nonphotosynthesizing, living, concrete substances, and so on. Concreteness and abstractness can be defined as degrees of specification. The fewer features associated with a word, the more abstract it is.

We have called our scale of abstraction a ladder; a better metaphor would be a tree, since at each descending step in the scale, more alternatives than one—i.e., branches—are available. Our ladder is only one of a very large number of ladders which merge at the top, as the following diagram shows:

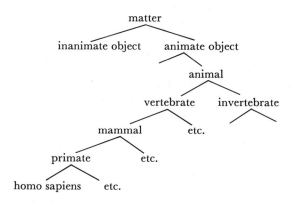

It would be incorrect to give the impression that all words fit into trees of abstraction as neatly as those just mentioned. The names for things in our immediate experience usually do so, but a great many common words do not. We do not seem to have terms adequate to fit into a tree the set including such words as "comment," "discuss," "explain," "describe," "remark," and "assert." Perhaps we could say that "asserting," "remarking," "commenting," and "discussing" are ways of *saying*, while "explaining" and "describing" are ways of *telling*, and "saying" and "telling" are both ways of *talking*. But what is the relation of "asserting" to "commenting" or "remarking"? Are they synonyms? If not, what features distinguish them from each other?

It is nevertheless the case that definition—including pointing—involves fitting words into some larger framework, showing their degree of abstraction, and showing how they differ from other words branching off from the same tree, i.e., showing what meaning features they have and do not have in common with other words on the same tree. An examination of the definitions in any good dictionary will show that, except in the rare case where words have synonyms, definitions are attempts to place words into a framework, the best analogy for which is a branching diagram.

Often for brevity a dictionary definition will be limited to a statement of the features which distinguish a word from the other words it could most easily be confused with, but a larger semantic framework is implied. Consider, for example, the definition of the word "dab": "1. to touch lightly and quickly, 2. to peck, 3. to pat with something soft and moist, etc." Clearly "touch" is more abstract than "dab." "Lightness" and "quickness" are features that distinguish "dabbing" from, say, "stroking" or "slapping." "Dab" fits into a tree in somewhat this way:

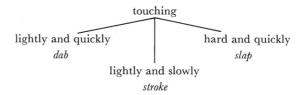

The dictionary definition of "dab" is a way of showing that "to dab" is less abstract than "to touch" and that it is different from other words on the same level of abstractness because of the specific combination of features it represents. "Dab" is only one of a large number of names for touching, each distinguished from the rest by one or more features of the English semantic system.

CHART IV. WORDS FOR "TOUCHING"

Semantic Features	dab	hit	press	slap	pat	push	peck	stab	rap	bang	beat
light	+	−	−	−	+	−	+	−	+	−	−
hard	−	+	+	+	−	+	−	+	−	+	+
quick	+	+	−	+	+	−	+	+	+	+	+
slow	−	−	+	−	−	+	−	−	−	−	−
flat	−	−	+	+	+	+	−	−	−	−	+(−)
blunt	+	+	+	−	−	−	−	−	+	+	+
sharp	−	−	−	−	−	−	+	+	−	−	−
object displaced	−	−	−	−	−	+	−	−	−	−	−
object stationary	+	+	+	+	+	−	+	+	+	+	+
object penetrated	−	−	−	−	−	−	+	+	−	−	−
noise produced	−	−	−	+	−	−	−	−	+	+	+
repeated	−	−	−	−	−	−	−	−	−	−	+
——— at	+	+	−	+	−	−	+	+	−	−	−
——— on	−	−	+	+	+	+	−	−	+	+	+

Trees based on semantic features invariably overlap with other trees, since the vocabulary reflects a total semantic system, the dissection of reality made by a whole language community. Thus the distinction "human —nonhuman" appears in many such trees, as the following example shows:

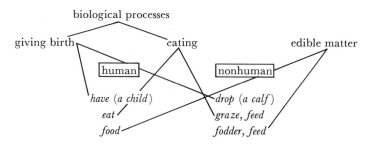

As the last two features included in the "touching" words chart show, the semantic features of words determine the other words with which they can co-occur. We have already noted that some verbs take only abstract objects, others take only human subjects, and the like. An adequate grammar must be one which is accompanied by a lexicon, or dictionary, that lists for each word all the semantic features which determine how the word may be used—not only with reference to the objects and ideas it can properly name, but also with reference to the features which must characterize the other words it combines with. Part of the rules included in Chapter Three are more correctly characterized as lexical—rather than syntactic— rules. For example, the division of nouns into mass and count is a semantic difference (though the semantic reference is not exact, since "furniture" is, for example, a mass noun while "ashes" is a count noun). The subdivisions of the verbs into transitive, intransitive, and linking might also be characterized as a semantic difference. The ideal grammar would be one which provided in the "deep" component a minimally developed set of rules representing the combination of grammatical categories (e.g., S ⟶ NP – Aux – VP). It would have to have a fully expanded dictionary, including as part of the description of each word the features that govern its combination with other words, including quasi-categorical rules like those governing the occurrence of transitive and intransitive verbs as well as rules relating to what have traditionally not been regarded as grammatical rules at all, such as the rules that forbid "He slowly stabbed his victim" or "He stabbed his victim with a brick"—i.e., rules which tell us that "stab" does not co-occur with adverbs containing the features "slow" or "blunt."

In literature and particularly in poetry it is possible to find instances of the co-occurrence of features that would not normally have that privilege. One device we use to shape old language to new purposes is the deliberate combination of words which otherwise do not co-occur. Thus one might deliberately create a sentence like "My chickens have been disappearing, and I think somebody has been disappearing them." The use of "disappearing" as a transitive verb has a degree of economy and interest which "causing to disappear" does not have. What are traditionally called "figures of speech" can usually be explained as the use of words in contexts which involve the deletion of features from one of the combining items or the addition of features to another. Metaphor is the deliberate application of a word with a given set of meaning features to a situation which has a partially different set of such features. A metaphorical term is typically a term made more abstract than it would normally be so that a broader range of experience is taken in. Thus if we say "her ingratitude cuts me to the quick," we are using "cut" instead of such more abstract terms as "hurts" or "injures." "Cuts," which normally has the meaning feature "applicable to physical objects" is moved closer to the top of the tree of abstraction and is applied to both physical and nonphysical objects. Its rhetorical effectiveness comes from the fact that it brings to the new situation some of the associations of its ordinary one: it makes the situation more tangible. Emotional injury acquires the vividness of a physical cut. As another example, one might speak of an idea as "embryonic." The term "embryonic" is lower on the tree of abstraction than a term like "rudimentary." It has the distinctive feature "applicable to animate objects." But calling ideas "embryonic" has the effect of extending the feature "animateness" to include ideas. An effective metaphor is one which produces a readjustment in a tree of abstraction of the type illustrated in the following diagram:

She cut me to the quick.

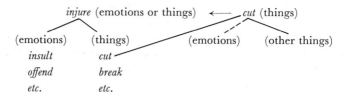

Other figures of speech involve much the same process. *Simile*, which makes use of the relational terms "like" and "as," involves associating terms with partially identical features in order to suggest the identity of normally distinct features. For example, to say that the "curled moon was like a little feather" is to apply to "moon" both the feature "curledness," usually applied only to manipulatable objects, and the feature "lightness, being supportable by air." *Synecdoche* provides even more obvious examples of shifts in the position of terms in the tree of abstractness: to call "food" "bread" is to move "bread" to a higher or more abstract position, with some such implication as "bread is the staff of life." Similar observations could also be made about *metonymy, hyperbole,* and *litotes.* The Old English poetic device called the *kenning* is a very interesting example of the use of the concept of changing degrees of abstractness for rhetorical effect. A *kenning* typically involves replacing a term with the combination of a term higher in the tree of abstractness and a lower-level differentiating term. Thus calling a sword a "battle flasher" is in effect choosing the higher term "flashing object" and the differentiating term "associated with battle" to replace the term "sword." The diagram below shows what takes place:

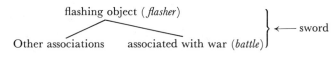

The same process is illustrated in the kennings "sea-steed" (ship), "swan road" (sea), "wave house" (ship), and "war wood" (spear).

Our discussion thus far has included several references to addition to the word stock of English. It may be well at this point to describe the processes of word formation in English in somewhat greater detail. We have already referred to the combination of free and bound forms, called *derivation*. In our discussion of nominalization by using a noun-marking suffix we illustrated a familiar kind of derivation: new nouns can be made up by adding suffixes such as "-ation," "-age," or "-ance," and the like to verbs. Nouns can, of course, also be made up with adjective or adverb bases and appropriate derivational suffixes such as "-ness," and "-ity." Verbs, adjectives, and adverbs can be made up in a similar way. Not all derivations change grammatical relationships: some of them are merely qualifiers, like "non-," "anti-," or "un-." Others signal direction or place, such as "ad-," "in-," "inter-," and "ex-." They signal degree, "per-"; repetition, "re-"; absence, "mis-," and far too many other meanings to mention here. Derived words are distinguished from *inflected* ones (that is ones marked for number, tense, possession, case, or comparison) by the fact that derived words are treated exactly like unitary words. "Mismatch," derived from two morphemes, is grammatically like "quarrel," containing only one. But inflected words do not behave like unitary words. They do not take inflections of their own. In phrases the inflected part normally has a function in the phrase as a whole rather than as part of a given word. Thus in the phrase "The boys are going," the "-s" of "boys" is related to the choice of "are" rather than "is," whereas the "mis-" of "mismatch" has no relevance outside the word itself.

In our discussion of the definition of the word, we considered the phenomenon of compounding, one of the most productive means of adding to the English word stock. This process has been in widespread use since Old English times, but it is, if anything, even more productive now. Relations that would once have been expressed by prepositions, certain verbs, or even full clauses are now commonly expressed by noun-noun sequences, many of which have become fully conventionalized compound words. The *Standard College Dictionary* lists thirty compounds beginning with "air," all written without hyphen or space. Most of them date from World War II or shortly before. The same dictionary also lists thirty-two sequences beginning with "air" which are written with space but which according to the definition given above must be considered unitary words. These are such words as "air brake," "air force," "air hole," "air lock," "air pocket," and "air power." The relations between "air" and the word following would have to be expressed in several different ways and at much greater length if the process of compounding were not available. An "air brake" is a brake that operates by means of air; and "air force" is a force that operates in the air; and "air hole" is a hole that admits air; and "air lock" is a chamber which holds air. "Air" may be the subject, object, or adverbially related adjunct of the succeeding word. These relations are usually describable in terms of grammatical transformations although it is sometimes the case that a compound in long use acquires a specialized meaning which cannot be explained in this way. For example, blackbirds need not be black, dimestores sell few items for a dime, and grammar schools teach little grammar.

The other principal means of adding to the English word stock is coinage; that is, making up words without using existing morphemes. Few words are coined, however, without some partial resemblance to already existing words. Some common types of coinage include acronyms, words formed with initials, such as NATO, UNESCO, WAVE, BAM, etc.; portmanteaus, words formed from submorphemic parts of existing words, such as "smog" from "smoke" plus "fog," "brunch" from "breakfast" plus "lunch," and "electrocute" from "electric" plus "execute"; reduplicated words, such as "chit-chat" from "chat" and "helter-skelter" probably from "heel"; clipped words, such as "flu" from "influenza" or "chum" from "chamber fellow"; and, last of all, words that appear to have been made up outright, such as "kodak" and "nylon."

Our discussion of meaning has been limited to the translation (or dictionary) meanings of words. But words have been conventionalized to signal much more than this. The following sets show that while words may have the same primary meaning, their secondary meanings may be quite different:

male sibling—brother—bud	attractive—cute
urinate—wee-wee—piss	in any case—anyway—anyhow
sir—Mr. Taylor—Jack—boy	attire—clothes—get-up

It is clear that several different kinds of secondary meanings are involved here. Some of these words give special information about how the speaker views the occasion. The choice of "male sibling" or "in any case" tells us that the speaker wishes to be considered educated (i.e., a member of the upper middle or upper class), that he regards his audience as peers, that he wishes to establish the occasion as formal and serious, and that his remarks are (or should appear to be) carefully prepared. The choice of "wee-wee" shows that the situation is to be viewed as involving an adult and a child;

speakers in the middle or lower-middle class are participating; the situation is informal, and there is no evidence of advance preparation. Since the word "wee-wee" is used in its ordinary way between an adult and a child, it becomes comic if used between adult peers. A speaker who uses "piss" marks himself as lower class. He tells his audience that he regards them as peers and the occasion as casual but neutral in tone; that is, not necessarily as either serious or comic. The choice of "cute" marks the speaker as a female of any age or male in his teens and twenties. The use of the term applied to his own clothes marks the male speaker as effeminate, but it may be applied to the appearance of a member of the opposite sex without this implication. "Anyway" and "anyhow" distinguish styles: "anyhow" marks the occasion as informal or casual and the situation as involving speaking, not writing. "Anyway" is neutral in these respects. The terms "sir" and "boy" as words of address are primarily signals of direction: "sir" points up to a superior while "boy" points in the opposite direction. The use of "Mr." as opposed to a nickname does the same thing. Thus the choice of one of several variants with the same translation meaning may suggest the following additional meanings: the speaker's view of himself (or information he gives away unknowingly): his age, his sex, his social class, his special subgroup (college student, jazz musician, religious sectarian, member of an occupational group, and the like). Furthermore, such a choice may indicate that the speaker views the situation as intimate, casual, formal, ceremonial, or neutral in these respects. He may also indicate whether he wishes to be taken seriously or not. Furthermore, in some instances he may show whether he wishes to be considered the superior, inferior, or peer of the person he is addressing. These secondary meanings can be tabulated as in Chart V.

Many words signal several of these meanings at once, as our illustrations above have shown. There is, of course, a kind of basic vocabulary which is neutral with respect to secondary meanings; that is, it is used by all speakers on all occasions. Such words include all the function words of English (prepositions, determiners, conjunctions, pronouns, auxiliaries) as well as names of common actions or occurrences, names of members of the family, names of objects commonly used, and numerals, colors, and basic value terms. (Almost all of these categories except numerals and function words have complementary sets of scientific and casual or comic names as well.) But there are few words in English totally lacking in secondary meanings; even scientific terms chosen for their explicitness of reference almost always have stylistic implications. This fact provides a fertile source of humor, intentional or otherwise. Shakespeare's most typical comic character was the foolish schoolmaster like Holofernes who in *Love's Labor's Lost* could say "I abhor such fanatical phantasimes, such insociable and point-device companions; such rackers of orthography as to speak dout, fine, when he should say doubt; det, when he should pronounce debt,—d, e, b, t, not, d, e, t,: he clepeth a calf, cauf; half, hauf; neighbor *vocatur* nebour; neigh ab-

CHART V.

Speaker-identifying words		*Illustrations*
Age	child	dolly, night-night
	teen	tough, bitchin'
	past 50	petticoat, fetch
Sex	male	broad, boobies, butt
	female	darling, cute, really?
Special Group	sectarian	saved, fornication, trespasses
	occupational	soffit, window-stool, mullion

Occasion-identifying words		*Illustrations*
Style-marking	*Spoken:*	
	intimate	Huh? Shut up. Quit it.
	casual	Maybe. What? "sorta"
	general	
	Written:	
	general	
	formal	sibling, in that case, multifarious
	ceremonial	Amen, whereas, inasmuch as
Relation-marking	adult-child	wee-wee
	peer-peer	
	superior-inferior	Sir, Mr., boy
Tone-marking	serious	alcoholic beverages
	comic	booze

breviated ne. This is abhominable—which he would call abbominable. It insinuateth me of insanie—*anne intelligis, domine?*" Dogberry and Verges in *Much Ado About Nothing* are guilty of similar showy language, theirs usually full of malapropisms as well. But even the humor of Dennis the Menace depends on the secondary meanings of words, as in "Mind if I sit down and yackety-yak for a spell?" and "It's Mrs. Ingram, Mom. She wants to mooch some more sugar."

Teaching Vocabulary

The expert user of a language is not necessarily the one who knows a lot of words. Rather, he is the person who knows enough words for his needs and who knows how to choose from among them precisely the ones he wants. The use of learned and unfamiliar words communicates little, and what it communicates is often irrelevant: it tells the listener that the speaker is out of touch at best and an exhibitionist at worst. Using words skillfully involves knowing their primary and secondary meanings and predicting accurately what effect they will have on hearers, given a particular occasion. Vocabulary learning that is limited to learning dictionary definitions is worse than useless; if students attempt to use words with no more familiarity with them than they can get in this way, they will surely not communicate successfully, and will almost inevitably embarrass themselves and their hearers.

Knowing words means first of all knowing where they fit in the kind of semantic hierarchy suggested above. A common bit of advice in schoolbooks is to look for synonyms in order to avoid repetition. Children are told to avoid repeating words like "say" and instead to use words like "comment," "remark," or "explain." The impression advice like this can give is that while variety in word choice is desirable precision is not. Commenting and remarking are not the same thing. They are both ways of *saying*, but commenting implies making an observation about something that has already been said, while remarking usually has the implication of freshness, the introduction of a new subject or a new point of view. It is also worth noting that both "comment" and "remark" have stylistic implications which are not shared by "say." "Say" is completely neutral, appropriate on all occasions and for all speakers. But "remark" and "comment" are hardly intimate or casual words. They belong to relatively careful, public speech, and they are more frequent in writing than in speaking. The indiscriminate use of so-called synonyms, particularly when this involves moving higher or lower in abstraction, can thus result in serious imprecision.

A concept which anyone interested in vocabulary building should master is the concept of concreteness and abstractness—the fact that words are different from each other in the fineness of the distinctions they make and that this difference makes it possible to view them as forming a kind of tree. This concept is readily teachable, and in my view it is one of the most valuable that beginning writers can acquire. In the process of making up such trees, children are forced to think through exact differences in the meanings of words. They have to ask questions like "Which of these terms is the most general?" "How much do these terms have in common?" "What is the exact difference between these terms?" "If these terms cannot always be used interchangeably, when do I use one and when do I use the other?" They can begin with easy sets like "vehicle," "car," "wagon," "boat," "yacht" or "make," "build," "erect," "compose," "assemble," and "shape." But at some time during their lower school or junior high studies they should begin to deal with problems like the relationship between "thinking," "discovering," "guessing," and "solving," or between "rights," "privileges," "liberty," "freedom," and "independence." The children will soon become aware of categories that are important in every English speaker's dissection of reality, including the distinctions between humanness and nonhumanness mentioned above, between animateness and inanimateness, between the physical and the nonphysical, and the like. But, most important, they will acquire a sense of the specific inclusiveness of a range of applicability of words, they will have an intellectual apparatus which they can apply in solving problems of word choice.

As for vocabulary building itself, that is, adding to one's list of familiar words, there is little that can be done in a formal way. The study of familiar prefixes, suffixes, and bases is widely practiced and no doubt useful. But adding words to one's vocabulary depends ultimately on making contact with increasingly more sophisticated language, using the dictionary for help in the early stages and finally acquiring a grasp of the range of applicability of new words. Requiring students to use new words in writing before they have fully understood the place of these words in the English semantic system does little good. Words must usually be in the recognition vocabulary for a long time before they are part of the production vocabulary. Having children keep a word notebook and finding answers to a specific set of questions is one way to help them focus on the right questions about new words. Their notation about a given word should include its dictionary definition, its stylistic range (written only? spoken only? casual? formal? etc.), and its tonal and directional implications. The source of this information must be context, since dictionaries give little more than a translation and stylistic judgment ("slang," "colloquial," etc.)

One thing the teacher can do is to provide these contexts systematically. That is, instead of forcing the child to wait for accidental recurrences of words he is in the process of learning, the teacher can provide those contexts, using such sources as concordances, quotation indexes, or subject indexes. And the children can use such sources on their own.

Mastery of the word stock of English, by the way, does not mean mastery of literary English alone. The skilled user of English is not the one who always talks like a book. On the contrary, he is the one who can exactly suit his vocabulary to the whole complex structure of communication— creating an occasion for his audience and showing them how to view him and what he has to say within that total context. Will Rogers and Adlai Stevenson were equally effective public speakers because each was able to make a precise statement in language consistent with his chosen image of himself and the occasion.

Topics for Investigation

1. Make a study of materials for learning foreign language vocabularies. You might include vocabulary card sets and the familiar "fourteen words a day" sort of material. How much of the language can a student intelligently expect to learn from such materials? What degree of command will he have of the words themselves (e.g., production as opposed to recognition command; knowledge of appropriateness and implications of the word in a variety of styles and situations)?

2. Compare the use of hyphens, white space, and no space with compound words in several dictionaries. Compounds with "air" or "space" make a good place to start. What differences do you find? What differences in theory might account for these differences in practice?

3. Making up new verbs by adding a particle (preposition or adverb) to a familiar verb is one of the most productive ways of adding to the English verb stock. Sometimes these verbs appear to signal nothing more than the meaning of the verb base plus the meaning of the particle, as in "knock out" or "fold up." But frequently the two parts have a wholly new meaning as in "give out" (succumb), "pull off" (perform successfully), "put off" (delay), or "put out" (extinguish). Should these units be regarded as two-part verbs, as verb plus completer, or verb plus preposition? What differences do you find among them? What are some of the most widely-used parts from which they are composed?

4. What differences in meaning usually accompany differences in stress and time such as those illustrated by the following phrases:

paper cutter	paper ribbon
elevator operator	elevator shoes
grape vine	grape wine
living room	living fossil

Should any of these be considered unitary words? What reasons would you give for classifying them as words or as phrases?

5. The words listed below have metaphorical extensions which are quite different from their primary meanings. In what contexts would the words be taken as metaphors? Do the differences in these semantic-grammatical contexts suggest that these "words" should be regarded as instances of homophones?

flush   sloth   gall   gather   fire

6. What possible misunderstandings could occur if someone attempted to teach a foreigner the meaning of the word "earth" by pointing to the ground? Can pointing be used satisfactorily to define such words as "trouble," "patience," or "similarity"?

7. Affixes may be called productive or nonproductive depending on whether or not they can be used to form new words. How would you classify these suffixes?

-able   -ness   -ity   -ive   -iance   -ize   -al

Do you notice any general semantic differences between words formed from productive suffixes and those formed with nonproductive ones?

8. What do the following words tell you about the speakers who use them?

grass (marijuana)	gook (oriental)
puke (vomit)	punk (teen-ager)
story book	fiddlesticks
abdomen	anthro (anthropology)

9. What can you say about the occasion (style, direction, tone) for which these words would be appropriate:

gimp (limp)	gobbledygook
platitude	in medias res
pal	phony
wow	jurist
split (depart)	fuss

Suggestions for Further Reading

For a fuller theoretical discussion of the definition of the word "word" see Charles F. Hockett, *A Course in Modern Linguistics* (New York: The Macmillan Company, 1958), Chapter 19. See also Leonard Bloomfield, *Language* (New York: Holt, Rinehart & Winston, Inc., 1933), pp. 207–47. Another valuable study is the article by Leonard Bloomfield, "Secondary and Tertiary Responses to Language," *Language*, XX (1944), 45–55; reprinted in H. B. Allen, *Readings in Applied English Linguistics* (New York: Appleton-Century-Crofts, 1964).

A richly detailed discussion of the origins of English words can be found in Stuart Robertson and Frederic Cassidy, *The Development of Modern English* (Englewood Cliffs, N.J.: Prentice-Hall, Inc., 1954), Chapters 7, 8, and 9. For an almost unlimited number of examples of the growth of the word stock of English in America see Thomas Pyles, *Words and Ways of American English* (New York: Random House, Inc., 1952).

The idea of semantic features and their relation to the rest of a grammar was discussed by Jerrold J. Katz and Jerry A. Fodor in "The Structure of a Semantic Theory," *Language*, XXXIX (1963), 170–210. Jerrold Katz and Paul M. Postal developed this principle further in *An Integrated Theory of Language Descriptions* (Cambridge: The M.I.T. Press, 1964). A full discussion of the relation of words to the things they name can be found in John B. Carroll, "Words, Meanings, and Concepts," *Harvard Educational Review*, XXXIV (1964), 178–202. See also Chomsky's discussion of lexicon in *Aspects of the Theory of Syntax*.

For a discussion of recent ideas on the nature of meaning, see Uriel Weinreich, "Explorations in Semantic Theory" in *Current Trends in Linguistics*, Vol. 3, Thomas A. Sebeok, ed. (The Hague: Mouton & Co., 1966).

Language Variation

Except for a handful of spellings, nothing from Old English survives unchanged today. We know that modern English is a descendent of Old English only because no other hypothesis could explain the multitude of similarities between the two languages. But if a speaker of Old English were to come to life again, he probably could not utter a single sentence that we would fully understand. Middle English, 500 years closer to the present, would not be much easier to understand, and even Elizabethan English would cause us serious difficulty. Futhermore, there is little likelihood that Chaucer could have understood King Alfred, or that Shakespeare would have understood Chaucer easily. Linguistic change in English has been going on at a fairly constant rate from the beginnings of the history of the language, and we can guess from the shape of some of its relatives such as Greek and Armenian that change was the rule long before English or its ancestor Germanic was identified by historians. Linguistic change is often viewed as a curiosity; people seem to get pleasure from reading strange etymologies or from hearing what Chaucer or Shakespeare sounded like. But the fact of the inevitability of linguistic change has very far-reaching consequences which are often not recognized. If linguistic change must go on, then it is going on now. And if it is going on now, then we are undoubtedly using forms that will shortly be archaic, while some of the innovations we hear around us will form part of the future shape of English. Our reverence for the standard and our scorn for the deviant must be tempered by the realization that if the world survives, English will change, and in a few hundred years modern texts will be studied with glosses and footnotes just as Shakespeare is today.

It is possible, of course, to argue that linguistic change should be stopped; and the many archaic features of our spelling system show that sometimes this argument can prevail. But it overlooks the fact that very little of language is under the control of any small group with agreed-upon principles and the power to enforce them. While our spelling was being held constant (as it has been in many respects since late Middle English), sound change was continuing at a steady rate, our grammar was losing old inflections and gaining new order rules, and our vocabulary was being rapidly augmented by borrowing and new formation. Furthermore, old words were being lost, and surviving words were undergoing drastic changes in meaning and applicability. It seems quite unlikely that any of these processes can ever be affected very much by deliberate planning. Only published English under the scrutiny of a handful of editors shows much sign of inhibited change.

Change is explained in several ways, some much more probable than others. It is said that languages change because their speakers are lazy; or, in more elegant terms, that there is a constant tendency to minimize the expenditure of energy in speaking. This tendency is one way to account for what is called assimilation, the fact that adjoining sounds tend to become more similar. The voicing of normally voiceless [t] in voiced contexts in English is a good example. "Conservation of energy" might also explain the simplification of initial consonant clusters in English: Old English had words beginning with *hr, hl, wr, wl* (all of which have been simplified) and, for many speakers, *hw* (as in "white") and *hy* (as in "humor") have gone the same way. But there is a basic illogic to this argument. It assumes that the language is moving from an older, maximally energy-consuming form to a newer, minimally energy-consuming one. Yet, judging from written texts at least, it does not appear that speaking Old English would have required a great deal more effort than does modern English. The fact is that along with the tendency toward simplicity there is a countertendency toward complexity. Modern English has simpler initial clusters but more complex final ones than Old English. We have introduced a distinction between voicing and voicelessness in the fricatives. And we have borrowed a very large number of foreign words which have immensely complicated our systems of both inflection and derivation. It might be argued that in the case of English the stronger tendency has been toward the *increase* of effort involved in the construction of sentences.

Some kinds of change are said to be explainable in anatomical terms. For example, the Negro vocal apparatus is said to be proportioned differently from that of the average Englishmen. This difference is supposed to have led to the dialect of the American Negro (and, some people say, to Southern dialect in general, since white children were in the care of Negro nurses). But it should be obvious that neither all Negroes nor all Englishmen are proportioned alike. There are undoubtedly greater differences within either group than there are between the two groups on the average. And innumerable histories of adopted children with ethnic backgrounds different from those of their adoptive parents show that racially related anatomical characteristics have nothing to do with the ability to learn a language perfectly.

An explanation some people find more satisfactory—and it is certainly more inclusive—is that languages, like everything else, are simply undergoing a process of decay. The argument is seldom applied wholesale, but it is certainly assumed in many common judgments of usage. The view can be stated very simply: the English language was once a very nearly perfect medium of communication, but it is rapidly going downhill, as innumerable instances of misused words and sloppy grammar all demonstrate. Robert Bridges' assertion that only stone buildings can be *dilapidated* suggests that he considers the older meaning of the word the only true one regardless of current usage, and Fowler's assertion that no matter how many people come to use a "wrong" form it will still be wrong, betray their acceptance of the view that languages can decay. But it is a different matter trying to identify the precise point in history at which English was perfect, or nearly so. Every form now in use was once "incorrect" in the sense that it was used by a minority of speakers; and schoolteachers seem always to have found fault with the direction the language was taking. There seems no way to show that modern English is less satisfactory as a means of communication than the English of Shakespeare, Chaucer, or King Alfred. The hasty inference that it is less satisfactory probably results from the fact that people seldom preserve for very many years literary documents that are ineffectively phrased or thought.

A better approach to explaining linguistic change is to begin with the question "What happens when a linguistic form changes?" The process of change must go on in somewhat this way: An innovation is introduced. It may be the accidental slip or deliberate creation of a single individual, or it may be a more-or-less simultaneous emergence among a whole group of speakers because of analogical features already in their language system. The innovation is adopted for a variety of social and linguistic reasons. If it is analogous to other structures within the language, its spread will be hastened. The same thing will happen if it fills a need created by cultural change. Various sociological factors are also involved such as the relative prestige—and imitability—of its users, or its function as a shibboleth of some in-group. Ultimately it may come to be regarded as the normal form.

Every sentence we utter contains an innovation of some sort since it is nearly impossible to exactly duplicate any utterance. The language tolerates some innovations more freely than others; when they do not affect communication, variations may be rather marked. For example, we can omit the *d* after nasals (as in "and" or "sand") rather freely; there are practically no instances in which this omission would lead to misunderstanding. But we could not omit initial *d* (as in "do" or "dice") without interfering seriously with our message. But every word tolerates some degree of variation.

Some innovations are nothing more than slips of the tongue. Others are unconscious reactions to the linguistic state of affairs. For example, the slip "growed" for "grew" shows the effect of the speaker's unconscious awareness of a general rule of English—that the past (even of words ending in /ow/ like "mow" or "show") is signalled by "-ed." This process, called analogy, has affected not only the inflections of English but also our processes of word formation and even our sound system. Once "-wise," as in the archaic "in no wise," had been introduced into English as a suffix in such words as "crosswise" and "sidewise," it began proliferating, and it is now used freely to make up such new words as "budgetwise" or "researchwise" or even "released-timewise"—sometimes to the dismay of purists. "-proof" has a similar history. Analogy also appears to be the explanation of the general simplification of initial consonant clusters mentioned above, and it can hardly be an accident that final "-nd" is being simplified to "-n" since "-mb" and "ng" have already lost their second consonant.

Another condition which may lead to linguistic change without the speaker's being particularly conscious of it is language and dialect interaction. Where almost an entire generation learn their community's principal language as a second language, their first language is almost certain to affect the second one. Yiddish influence on the English of many native speakers in New York is easily discernible, and second or third generation Scandinavian-Americans in the upper Midwest often show obvious traces of their language heritage. Dialect mixture may very well account for the disappearance of the distinction between /a/ and /ɔ/ in Western American English. The western states have been settled by Americans from the upper and lower Midwest and the South. While all these dialect areas distinguish [a] from [ɔ], they do so in different words. Upper-Midwesterners typically say [fag] but [gɔd], while lower-Midwesterners say [fɔg] and [gad]. Southerners typically have [ɔ] only as a diphthongized form. The consequence of the mixture of these pronunciations through the migration of their users would almost inevitably be the loss of distinctiveness of the vowels in question, which seems to be exactly what has happened.

Language change, of course, also reflects cultural change. Its effects are most noticeable in the area of semantics, though they may be felt in the grammar and in the formal features of the lexicon as well. The interrelations of language and culture are very complex, and there can be little doubt that each affects the other. The same shift in social organization that led the Quakers to substitute "thee" and "thou" for the polite and formal "you" and "ye" ultimately caused the English language to lose the old singular, familiar forms altogether, with the polite, plural forms becoming generalized. But the other European languages retained pronoun differences as a grammatical means of distinguishing between familiarity and politeness. Shifts in word meaning are certainly the most common reflection of value shifts in a society. The word "compromise," for example, at one time had a favorable connotation; a compromise was a rational man's way of achieving a nonviolent settlement. But now, probably reflecting a new militancy and belligerency in American attitudes, it suggests appeasement, an undesirable yielding to pressure.

The kinds of language innovation described so far generally occur without the speaker's being aware of what is happening. But some kinds of linguistic change are quite deliberate and conscious. Borrowing is the most obvious example. Borrowing is always related to cultural change. In the history of English, we have borrowed names for borrowed things. Our vocabulary of jurisprudence, war, cookery, and costume is mostly of French origin and it betrays the source of most of our ideas on these topics. Our vocabulary of the sciences is mostly from Greek; of music from Italian; of art from various Romance languages. But our words for familiar, ordinary life, common foods, the trades, farming, the members of the family, the parts of the body, and the numbers have all been with us since prehistory. Thus our borrowed vocabulary reflects the diffusion of culture from continental Europe to England and America.

The second kind of conscious and obvious linguistic change is deliberate prescription. The traditional rules for "shall" and "will," which appear never to have reflected actual usage, are an instance of this. The insertion of the *b* in "debt" and "doubt" was a case of tampering with otherwise regular spelling. Premature attempts at regularizing, such as the prescription of "dived" for "dove," "lighted" for "lit," and "pleaded" for "pled" illustrate the grammarian's impatience with ordinary usage. The schools have done much to foster this kind of innovation. They have legislated against prepositions at the ends of sentences, split infinitives, and gerunds without possessives—apparently without any basis in usage. Recent studies, such as those by William Labov, mentioned above, have shown that a preoccupation with and need for prescriptions of this sort is related to membership in the lower middle class, but even upper class schools, especially those for girls, have often imposed an artificial pronunciation standard and a bookish, archaic grammar and vocabulary.

Innovation in language is thus both a conscious and an unconscious phenomenon. It may result from forces of which the speakers are totally unaware, or the speakers may deliberately initiate a linguistic change. But only a tiny minority of the innovations which occur actually become part of the speech habits of the whole English-speaking world. Those that survive do so because of complex and interrelated sociological and linguistic conditions. And many of those that survive do so only among small groups of speakers. An innovation can "catch on" only among a group of speakers who are actually in face-to-face contact. Thus speaker A's innovation may be taken up by his intimate B, who may in turn transmit it to his intimates C and D, who may in their turn use it in conversation with their mutual acquaintance A (perhaps to his gratification). But the chain does not necessarily keep going on to speakers F, Q, X, Y, and Z. It is not true that all speakers of English are linked to each other by equally numerous chains of contacts. In fact, most of us belong to groups whose members do by far the largest share of their conversing with each other. Their contacts outside are of the most tenuous kind—buying and selling, paying taxes, listening to (but not answering) addresses, and the like. Thus the inevitability of linguistic change coupled with the relative isolation of speakers of English for social, geographical, or personal reasons must inevitably lead to the emergence of special varieties of English.

Regional variation in English has been far more thoroughly studied than has social variation. Extensive research has been carried out and maps have been drawn of the speech areas of both England and the United States. In each country the hypothesis that weakness in lines of communication leads to dialect variation has been fully demonstrated. The northeastern American cities oriented toward England adopted certain sound changes that occurred in London such as the lost "r" after vowels and the centralizing of the vowel of "bath," while the American back country never adopted these innovations. The same differences in orientation and way of life that led to the Civil War have created the boundary that divides Southern from Midland dialect. Old isolating factors, such as orientation toward a certain city, may be reflected in settlement patterns westward. The upper Midwestern states have a dialect much like that of western New England and upstate New York, while the lower Midwestern states divide into two Midland dialect belts reflecting settlement straight westward from Pennsylvania and from the southern border states. The west of the United States shows the fanning out of the Midland dialect, with a considerable mixture of North and South Midland forms and traces of both Inland Northern and Southern dialect.

Regional differences in English show up most clearly in pronunciation. It is easy to tell where the ordinary New Yorker is from, and speakers from Eastern New England and the Southern coast also betray their origins by their vowels and consonants. It is most obviously differences in pronunciation which the traveler from Boston to Atlanta or Minneapolis to New Orleans notices. America has not developed a pronunciation "standard" which is regarded as equally prestigeful in every part of the country. A politician with a Yankee dialect would have a slim chance of winning in Georgia, and a Southern dialect is no help at all in Pennsylvania. Recent studies have shown that the beginnings of such a standard may be appearing, at least in the North; but at present it is not possible to prescribe a system of pronunciation which will assure its user of acceptance anywhere.

Some items of vocabulary and grammar are also more specifically related to region than to class or style, but there are very few of these. There is a regional vocabulary of cookery, common tools and implements, and rural life, but the *Linguistic Atlas of the United States* shows that these words are often known only to people in their middle years and older. Younger people tend to adopt the national words (usually commercial ones) for such things as cottage cheese, pancakes, sour milk, corn tassels, peanuts, and dairy barns. Regional words survive best when the things they name are specifically regional, such as sugar bushes, arroyos, century plants, and chinooks. It seems to be true in the case of vocabulary that the commercial media supply links between otherwise isolated segments of our society, and that these links are strong enough to permit the diffusion of a national vocabulary. The items of grammar that are specifically regional are even more rare. They consist primarily of verb forms, pronoun forms, a few phrase patterns, such as "I want out," and matters of intonation. And most regional grammatical forms are not characteristic of all the speakers in a given region but rather of members of the lower social classes. Instances like "y'all" which is regional but not class related are very rare.

Social class variation is the least studied but unquestionably the most important kind of dialect variation in English. It affects pronunciation, grammar, and vocabulary. It is both an effect and a cause of the social stratification of our society. For some speakers of lower class dialect, adopting that of the middle class may present many of the same problems as learning a foreign language—and may be one of the major labors in the Herculean series that must be gone through before one can improve his status in our society. Social class dialect relates to regional dialect in complicated ways. Regional dialects can become class dialects as migrants from a given region and belonging to a similar socioeconomic level take up residence in a new area. Thus Negro dialect, which was originally Southern regional dialect with some pidginization, has become a social class dialect in the ghettos of the North and West. South Midland dialect, spoken without class stigmatization in its original area, became "Okie" in California, and is still considered a mark of inferior status there.

Ordinarily the dialect of the "old families" is the high prestige dialect of an area. Newcomers are almost certain to be lower in status than these families, and the dialect they bring with them will be regarded as inferior. The author's research suggests that migrants from the South Midland and South who have achieved any degree of social and economic success in California have generally adopted the Middle and North Midland forms that predominate there. The exceptional cases are such people as used-car dealers or funeral directors whose trade comes to a considerable extent from among the unassimilated migrants and who have found it to their advantage to maintain a "back home" dialect. Sometimes, however, a dialect area will be so swamped with migrants from a new area that the dialect of the migrants will become the prestige dialect. Research in the San Francisco and Puget Sound areas, in which the original settlement was predominantly from New England but which were later settled by very large numbers of Midwesterners, has shown that a New England dialect carries no prestige, and, indeed, in the case of San Francisco it has been regarded as a handicap.

Besides transplanted regional dialects, the sources of social class language variation are a foreign language substratum (which probably accounts for the use of a stop consonant for the fricative in words like "them" and "they" in lower class dialects of the Northeastern cities), and the kind of accidental, cumulative variation discussed above. It is undoubtedly this last kind of variation which accounts for the largest share of the features which distinguish American social class dialects. It is easy to tell by a man's speech whether he is a member of a family that is accustomed to wealth and education or a half-literate, impoverished migrant farm laborer. Yet the difference is not primarily one of formal education. It is true that the educated man's vocabulary will very likely attest to his wider reading and that he will avoid the shibboleths of "illiterate" or "vulgar" English— "ain't," "he don't," and the like. But his education will barely have touched on most of the features that mark his speech as representing his class—his vowel and consonant system, his intonation, his favorite sentence types, his choice among equally explicit and established English words. These things he will have learned entirely by association with the other members of his class in the same way that the farm laborer will have learned his speech patterns.

Social class dialect involves all aspects of language. It affects pronunciation in both obvious and subtle ways. The pronunciation of [r] after vowels in New York City seems to be related to social class, and members of the middle and lower middle classes are highly conscious of this fact and take pains to affect [r] in careful speech. The diphthong [æy] in words such as "laugh," "bath," "dance," and "pass," is a mark of low prestige in most parts of the North and West, and many speakers rather consciously avoid it. In the South Midland area some speakers are careful to avoid raised and fronted final unstressed vowels in words like "camera" (sometimes pronounced [kæmeri]). This principle seems to account for the hypercorrect pronunciation of "Missouri" as [mizurə]. And there are, of course, lower and higher prestige pronunciations of certain words quite apart from the sound system as a whole. For many speakers the pronunciation [ænt] for "aunt" is a mark of inferior status, as are [iyðər] for "either" and numerous others.

But vowels and consonants account for only part of the pronunciation differences that relate to social class. There are also the extended features of speech—the patterns of intonation, the general level of tension, the degree of assimilation, and sometimes even the speed of English which mark a speaker as belonging to a higher or lower class. These features are extremely difficult to describe in general terms. And, like other features of pronunciation, they differ somewhat from region to region in their relevance to status. But it is probably the case in general that upper class speech is more tense. It tolerates considerable assimilation, but probably not as much as does lower class speech. It is probably in general somewhat faster. A precise and carefully recorded statement of these differences, however, is yet to be made.

Grammar is what most conspicuously marks class dialect, if school materials are to be trusted. Labeling grammatical constructions as "educated," "cultivated," "vulgar," "a barbarism," "illiterate," "dialectal," and even "preferred" is unmistakably labeling them according to the supposed social status of their users. "Preferred" can only mean "preferred by people of high status." "Education" and "cultivation" are the products of upper class wealth and values, and "vulgarity" and "illiteracy" are the products of the lack of these things. There is a well-known list of shibboleths including "don't" for "doesn't," "seen" for "saw," "was" for "were," "laid" for "lay," "ain't" and dozens of others which are quite specifically labeled as lower class by the schools. Most of these are undoubtedly labeled correctly. In addition, however, such larger grammatical considerations as frequency of certain types of transformations, favorite phrase structures, degree of embedding, and degree of reduction seem to be class related. There is little evidence as yet to determine precisely which of these larger grammatical components are related to social class, however.

Vocabulary also has a great deal to do with status, as has been noted in an earlier chapter. The difference between, say, "gut" and "abdomen" is not primarily a matter of style; that is, it is quite unlikely that the same person would choose one for one occasion and the other for another. "Gut" (except in medical contexts) is a lower class word (as distinguished from "guts," which relates to style, not class). The middle and upper class variants include "stomach," "belly," "abdomen," "tummy," and the like, depending on the occasion and the speaker's sex and age. Names for bodily processes and for sexual behavior, particularly incest and deviation, vary greatly from class to class, and terms accepted as perfectly ordinary by the lower class speaker may seem excessively blunt or offensive to members of the middle classes. A survey of the attitudes of college students, including representatives of the middle and upper middle classes, showed that almost every informant regarded the word "fuck" as very offensive, yet it is in common use among lower class speakers and it seems to have much weaker negative connotations for them. Some subtler class-related vocabulary differences are those between "right along" and "continuously," "farther" and "further," "plenty" and "sufficiently," and the like.

It goes without saying that the very large social classes usually identified by sociologists as Upper, Upper Middle, Middle, Lower Middle, and Lower do not account for all the social subgroupings in American society. There are innumerable minor groupings of varying degrees of exclusiveness. The greater the exclusiveness, the greater the uniformity of language within the group and the greater its difference from the language of outsiders. A small, extremely exclusive religious sect such as the Plymouth Brethren tends to develop marked language peculiarities, usually in the special definitions of words. For example, among this sect at the time the author was observing them the word "exercise" had come to mean "choice," the word "assembly" had come to mean something like the Calvinist "elect," and "freedom" meant complete commitment to the faith. Other exclusive groups with highly developed in-vocabularies include jazz musicians, members of motorcycle clubs, users of "mind-expanding" drugs, the various subgroups of the criminal underworld, and, of course, constantly emerging and dissolving groups like the Beats and the Hippies.

Language varies according to a third principal condition which we will call *style*. *Style* is what is sometimes called level of discourse; that is, the style of an utterance can be classified on a scale moving from spontaneous, intimate speech to wholly planned, ceremonial writing. Every composition student has had to learn that written English is not spoken English, and everyone who has had to prepare remarks to be made in public has discovered that neither a written style nor a spontaneous spoken one will serve his purpose exactly. The division between written and spoken English is the most obvious. Pronunciation cannot be compared of course, but the grammar and vocabulary of these styles are markedly different. Even minor matters of grammar may be conventionalized to serve one purpose but not the other. "For" as a conjunction seems to occur only in writing; "well" as a sentence introducer seems to occur only in speech. "Anyhow" and "anyplace" are exclusively spoken; "anyway" and "anywhere" must replace them in writing. Compare the uses of "sort of" and "rather," "guess" and "suspect," "have got" and "have," "lay" and "lie," "lots of" and "many," "most" and "almost," "real" and "very," and far too many more to list here. These are in part matters of grammatical class shift, in part matters of word choice. The following series of quotations will illustrate what appear to be the major subtypes of spoken and written English.

1. Ceremonial Written English

From many prayer books:

> O God who hast safely brought us to the beginning of this day, keep us in the same with thy mighty power and grant that we fall into no sin, neither run into any kind of danger, but that all our doings, being ordered by thy governance, may be righteous in thy sight, through Jesus Christ our Lord. Amen.

2. Formal Written English

LSA Journal, Language, XL (1964), p. 329:

> George Melville Bolling was born in Baltimore on 13 April 1871, into a family of great distinction in the life of the south and of the country. From this background he derived his many social gifts as well as his interest in politics. While he was happily engaged, until a year before his death, in scholarly reading and writing, ever eager to discuss it with some of his friends, and visitors, others knew and

admired him as a player of chess and a renowned bridge expert; again, he might at any time be discovered at his desk, writing to some governmental acquaintance on an issue of the day. He was no stranger to Washington, and he liked to speak of the time when the Wilson administration, to which he was attracted by bonds of kinship and political preference, called on him in his capacity as a Hellenist to give an opinion on the history and ethnic complexion of Thrace.

3. General Written English

NEA Journal, January, 1965, p. 8:

Here is a text from Yale's late president, Whitney Griswold: "Every basic institution bears a direct responsibility for society's moral health. The university bears a large and exceptionally important part of this responsibility."

What can we say of the moral health of our universities? Not long ago a foreign observer remarked, "You Americans are so obsessed with the luxuries of life that you are forgetting the necessities." What he had in mind might have been what has been termed the "good nonlife" in America, the way our culture makes the middle class safe, polite, obedient, and sterile.

A couple of centuries ago most college graduates went into the service of either the church or the state. That may explain, in part, why at the founding of our nation, when we had a total population of only three million (less than that of Los Angeles County today) we turned out a generation of statesmen named Washington, Hamilton, Franklin, Jefferson, Adams—and you could go on to name a list as long as your arm.

Not long ago a student came to me with one of those interminable questionnaires. He was going to study the student values at Yale. So I said, "All right, if you can't decide on any and you can't live any, I suppose you can always study them."

4. General Spoken English

Mark Twain, "How to Tell a Story":

I do not claim that I can tell a story as it ought to be told. I only claim to know how a story ought to be told, for I have been almost daily in the company of the most expert storytellers for many years.

There are several kinds of stories, but only one difficult kind— the humorous. I will talk mainly about one. The humorous story is American, the comic story is English, the witty story French. The humorous story depends for its effect upon the manner of the telling; the comic story and the witty story upon the matter.

The humorous story may be spun out to great length, and may wander around as much as it pleases; but the comic and witty stories must be brief and end with a point. The humorous story bubbles gently along, the others burst.

The humorous story is strictly a work of art—high and delicate art—and only an artist can tell it; but no art is necessary in telling the comic and the witty story; anybody can do it. The art of telling a humorous story—understand, I mean by word of mouth, not print—was created in America, and has remained at home.

5. Casual Spoken English

The Fresno Bee, January 5, 1965, p. 5C:

It wasn't too terrible, just awfully crowded and we never had enough to eat. The trip by ship to Goa, India, nine months later, was much worse. It took a month. The ship was unbelievably crowded and it was terribly hot. But what I minded most of all was not being able to bathe. Just before we got there, I knew I just couldn't stand it any more. I bribed a steward to let me bathe. I paid him $50 for that bath in a dirty tub. Can you imagine that?

. . . Actually I think it was those coffees that won the election for him, those and the door-to-door campaigning he did. He did get so tired, though. One time he rang a doorbell and when the housewife answered he was so beat all he could get out was "I _____." When he told me about it I asked, "What did she answer? 'Me, Jane,' and pull you inside?"

6. Intimate Spoken English

James Baldwin, *Blues for Mister Charlie* (New York: Dell Publishing Co., Inc., 1964), p. 43:

Richard: You want to dance?
Juanita: No, not now.
Richard: You want something to eat?
Juanita: No. Richard?
Richard: Yeah?
Juanita: Were you *very* sick?
Richard: What d'ya want to know for?
Juanita: Like that. Because I used to be your girl friend . . .
Richard: You were more like a boy than a girl, though. I couldn't go nowhere without you. You were determined to get your neck broken.
Juanita: Well, I've changed. I'm now much more like a girl than I am like a boy.
Richard: You didn't turn out too bad, considering what you had to start with.
Juanita: Thank you. I guess.
Richard: How come you ain't married by now? Pete, now, he seems to be real fond of you.

Several features mark quotation one as ceremonial English: its high percentage of ready-made phraseology (how many of the same phrases are used almost unchanged in other prayers?); its archaic vocabulary; its carefully balanced combination of phrases; its unmistakable markers "O God" and "Amen." It is also interesting that it consists of only one sentence (and one main clause) containing fifty-eight words. By contrast, quotation two, formal written English, has a mean sentence length of 39.7 words. Its vocabulary is not archaic, and little of its phraseology is ready made. But it is unmistakably formal. Notice, for example, its use of full (rather than reduced) phrases as in "a family of great distinction" rather than "a distinguished family." Notice its use of markedly literary phrases such as "bonds of kinship" and "ethnic complexion." Notice also the use of "ever" in an affirmative, declarative phrase, a combination that does not occur in speech. The slightly archaic "discovered" in the sense "observed" or "seen" further marks this passage as formal and literary. Notice the careful balance of the third and fourth sentences, each beginning with a phrase stating an idea in a general way followed by an elaborate expansion and qualification of it. The paragraph has the marks of patient effort, of careful drafting and revision, of the deliberate choice of bookish and faintly archaic forms, all contributing to an effect quite appropriate to the obituary of a philologist, which this is.

It is to be contrasted to quotation three, general written English. This paragraph has a mean sentence length of 18.1 words and a median of eleven words. It contains several markedly informal words and phrases such as the abrupt introductory "here," the use of "a couple of" instead of "two," "turned out" instead of "produced," the metaphor "as long as your arm," the familiar "one of those interminable questionnaires," and the use of "so" as a sentence introducer. The paragraph also contains reduced constructions that could not occur in formal or ceremonial English, such as "Yale's president" for "the president of Yale," "society's moral health," "the way our culture makes . . ." for "the way in which our culture makes . . .," the omission of a whole clause—perhaps "that we all know about"— after "one of those interminable questionnaires." Instead of balanced declarative sentences, we have strikingly different sentence types: a fragment for the introductory sentence, a question at the beginning of the second paragraph, direct discourse in the last paragraph. Notice also the omission of explicit relational words between the sentences of the third and fourth paragraphs, despite the fact that in each instance causal connections are to be inferred. The paragraph would almost be speakable—except for some quite unconversational features, such as the rhetorical question of paragraph two, the rather elaborate series which concludes the same paragraph, and the parenthesis of paragraph three, which produces an interruption that could not be bridged in speech.

The differences between this quotation and the one from Mark Twain are slight. Mark Twain's remarks are said to be part of a speech, but they show some marks of composition, such as the use of "for" as a coordinating conjunction. But in general this quotation sounds more like speech than writing. Notice the high percentage of simple main sentences without very complex embedding or expansion. Notice also that most of the sentences are "compound," that is, combinations of main sentences connected by "and," "but," "for," or a semicolon. The average number of words per sentence in this passage is 21.5; but the mean number of words per main clause is only 10.2, by contrast with quotation three, in which the mean is 18.1. Aside from sentence simplicity (and the absence of explicit relation words), little distinguishes the Mark Twain speech from general written English. Quotation five, on the other hand is marked as speech in many ways: by a nonrhetorical question addressed to a listener; by the use of exclusively spoken vocabulary such as "too" for "very," "stand" for "endure," "actually" as a sentence introducer, "so" for "very," and "beat" for "exhausted." Other features characteristic of speech but not writing include the absence of relation words and the repetition of the subject "I." As in most spoken English, the sentences are short, the mean being 11.1 and the mean for main clauses being 9.4. It is principally the vocabulary and the absence of relation words that mark this as more casual than quotation four.

The sixth quotation, intimate spoken English, is characterized primarily by maximum sentence reduction. In the exchange of conversation, only those elements are added which are not repetitions of what has gone before. Other marks of intimacy are the interrupted sentences such as "Because I used to be your girl friend . . ." and "I guess," suggesting that the other speaker knows details that need not be repeated. The mean sentence length is only 5 words. There is almost a complete absence of sentence-connecting words. The use of contractions and such expressions as "like that," "yeah," "real" for "very," "you want" for "do you want," and "bad" for "badly" contribute to the impression of intimate speech. One sentence is rather conspicuously out of place: "You were determined to get your neck broken." "Determined" is too literary, and "broke" would certainly be more consistent with the style of the rest of the passage than "broken." In summary, at least the following features seem to distinguish styles in English: sentence length and main clause length, sentence fullness as opposed to sentence reduction, ratio of subordinate (or reduced subordinate) clauses to sentences, special vocabularies, and special grammatical forms.

Which of the varieties of English discussed thus far is the so-called standard English of the usage handbooks? None—although the handbooks have in general selected a widely useful style and class variant, and perhaps even a regional pronunciation variant. The schoolbooks in general prescribe a style characteristic of general or formal written English (depending on the age and relative conservatism of the book). To the extent that written styles reflect class dialects, this style reflects that of the upper middle and upper class, although the schoolbooks are not unaffected by the phenomenon of lower middle class hypercorrection. The only widely prescribed variety of spoken English, standard broadcast speech, is a way of pronouncing what is in fact written English for use on radio and television. It is a somewhat artificial variant of Inland Northern dialect. It is the dialect affected by most readers of news reports and commercials across the country, but not necessarily by either outstanding actors or commentators. Besides having the ordinary characteristics of Inland Northern English, this dialect is characterized by the absence of assimilation between words and by hyper-articulation, particularly of consonants, within words.

Language Variation and the Teaching of English

The foregoing discussion must have made it clear that for the schools to try to stamp out all varieties of English except "standard" can only lead to disaster. In the first place, there *is* no standard if by standard one means a single variety of English suitable for all persons on all occasions. Furthermore, no variety of English can be called intrinsically better than any other. Each variety of English is exactly suited to the situation in which it is normally used. To use a bookish style on a casual occasion or an upper class dialect in a lower class setting is to invite at best amusement and at worst failure to communicate. Thus every speaker's native dialect is essential for him unless he wants to cut himself off completely from his class and regional origins. The case of Eliza Doolittle must be considered exceptional! As has been pointed out above, a skilled user of English is confident, fluent, and versatile. Assisting him in gaining command of dialects and styles he has not mastered should be a matter of increasing his versatility, not destroying his confidence or fluency in his native language.

Unhappily, Americans often evaluate others on the basis of superficial features of their language. Research has shown that middle class Americans are most willing to hire and to associate with people who speak their own class dialect. They also tend to reject speakers of regional dialects different from their own, particularly if those regional dialects also have social class associations. Thus if it is part of the task of the schools to prepare children for the highest achievement they are capable of in our society, then it is in part their task to help the children escape the stigmatization that may come from their commanding only a lower class dialect in a casual spoken style. There seem to be two dangers involved in any attempt to change children's dialect. On the one hand, there is the danger of destroying their fluency, of making them so conscious of form that their speech—and writing—become strained, overly careful, and stiff. There is the related danger of destroying their confidence, of persuading them, perhaps only indirectly, that their speech is actually inferior to what they are being taught. This lack of confidence appears to be the principal cause of the decreasing imaginativeness and creativity of children's language as they proceed through school. Their confidence is so shaken that they will put down on paper only those simple sentences and familiar words and phrases that they are sure they can produce correctly. The second principal danger facing the teacher setting out to expand children's command of "higher" dialects and style is hypercorrection. Teachers are often likely to be sensitive about matters of language correctness, eager to observe a standard and to impose it on others. But it is not the case that every textbook prescription necessarily reflects actual written or spoken usage. Furthermore, the best English typically shows evidence of experimentation with forms outside the rigid conventions of class and style. An issue of any magazine attracting excellent writing contains abundant examples of this sort of thing. The word "busted" (= either broken or arrested) has appeared repeatedly in serious essays in general English, for the very good reason that no other word in English means quite the same thing, but it is still forbidden by most handbooks. The teacher of style must be always on guard against the danger of prescribing too much, of discouraging originality and experimentation. Above all, he must guard against the outright inaccuracy of forbidding or requiring forms which are not really forbidden or required in the style he is teaching.

The teacher's job, then, is to increase versatility without shaking confidence or impairing fluency. His general approach must be first of all to expose his children to enough examples of the varieties of English that they come to recognize the principle that different occasions have different language conventions. He will have to use the general principle that the pupils should do the maximum amount of sentence production. But merely having them write sentences will hardly teach what he proposes unless he wants to do a great deal of error analysis, and error analysis is usually counterproductive. Instead of increasing students' versatility it only decreases their fluency and confidence. Instead, he must give them ready-made examples which they reshape in various ways using as much as possible of what they have been given. Thus they can do sentence combinations with connectives, sentence permutations, sentence reductions and expansions, all leading them to make up new sentences while providing them with as much as possible of the material to make them of. More advanced activities can include the writing of précis and summaries and of converting spoken stories or talks to written ones and vice versa.

A key point to remember is that the students must at all times be clear about the fact that the language they are learning is related to occasions. They should not be asked to talk in a written style or write in a spoken one. They should always have a clear idea of what audience they are composing for, what level they are choosing, what tone they are trying to achieve. Versatility does not come from language practice apart from the situations in which language is really used.

Topics for Investigation

1. What evidences of linguistic change can you find in current writing and speech? Can you find any evidence of sound change? What kind of change is most noticeable?

2. Take at random any passage consisting of several sentences of general written English. How much of its form is included in the set of prescriptions usually taught in the schools? What accounts for the regularity of the rest of its grammar?

3. Make an analysis of the grammatical errors on any set of student papers. What hypothesis can you make as to their cause? Are any of these errors evidence of linguistic change?

4. What are the features of grammar and pronunciation most characteristic of ghetto Negro dialect? (A good way to find out is to visit a lower-grade playground in a ghetto school.) What evidence do you find of the following: regularity in grammar not characteristic of "higher" class dialects? different meanings of words, particularly secondary meanings? differences in the inventory of vowels and consonants? differences in extended pronunciation features including patterns of intonation?

5. The words "agribusiness" and "motorcade" are examples of incorrect morphemic analysis of existing words providing the components of new words. Can you find other examples of this phenomenon?

6. How have the secondary meanings of the following words changed in recent times?

appeasement   pacification   welfare   democracy

7. Make a study of any exclusive social group, such as a religious sect or an extremist political group. What evidence do you find of the development of language features limited to the group? What aspects of language seem to have been affected most?

8. Using Kurath's *Word Geography of the Eastern United States*, determine which dialect area your own vocabulary resembles most closely. Does your vocabulary reflect your geographical origin accurately? If it does not, what could explain the error?

9. Listen for dialect jokes and comic references to dialect. What dialects do you find ridiculed most? Are some dialects treated more kindly than others—i.e., do their speakers come off better in humorous stories? What features of dialect do dialect storytellers usually emphasize?

10. Make a study of labeling in any list of "Words Commonly Misused," such as that in the *College Handbook of Composition* by Wooley, Scott, and

Bracher. How many different labels (e.g., "preferred," "informal," and the like) do you find? Are these labels related to social class or style or both? What levels of style and social class seem to be recommended?

11. What level of style predominates in the following journals: *Life, Transaction, Language, Reader's Digest, Ramparts*? Does your study of these magazines lead you to believe that more than three levels of written English might be recognized?

12. The chart below makes use of the secondary meaning features discussed in an earlier chapter. Check the squares which correctly relate each locution to inferences that can be made about the speaker and the occasion.

	Speaker							Style						Relation			Tone		
	Age	Sex	Class	Region	Special Ident.			Spoken	Written								Serious	Comic
	Child / Teen / Adult / Aged	M / F	Upper / Middle / Lower	NE / SE	Central / College / Jazz / Sectarian / Occupational			Intimate / Casual / General	General / Formal / Ceremonial				Child–Adult / Peer–Peer / Inferior–Superior			Argument / Exposition / Description	Satire / Humor	
get-up (costume)																	
screw (copulate)																	
spell-binder																	
darn!																	
Sir																	
blow your mind																	
Hi!																	
therefore																	
Well . . .																	
Amen																	
buggy (car)																	
tuff																	
Georgie																	
uh-uh																	
for (conj)																	
anyhow																	
be saved																	
heuristic																	
cute																	
anthro																	
go potty																	

Suggestions for Further Reading

The regional dialects of English are described briefly and clearly in C. E. Reed, *Dialects of American English* (New York: The World Publishing Company, 1967). The most extensive studies of American dialect are limited to the states east of the Mississippi. These include Hans Kurath, *Handbook of the Linguistic Geography of New England* (Providence: Brown University Press, 1939); Hans Kurath and R. I. McDavid, *Pronunciation of English in the Atlantic States* (Ann Arbor: University of Michigan Press, 1961); Hans Kurath, *A Word Geography of the Eastern United States* (Ann Arbor; University of Michigan Press, 1949); and E. B. Atwood, *Verb Forms in the Eastern United States* (Ann Arbor: University of Michigan Press, 1953). Western dialect studies can be found in scattered articles in *American Speech* and in the *Publication of the American Dialect Society*.

The social dialectology of the United States is only beginning to be studied. Some important titles now in print include William Labov, *The Social Stratification of English in New York City* (Washington D.C.: Center for Applied Linguistics, 1966); and Jean Malmstrom, *Language in Society* (New York: Hayden Book Company, 1965). Some influential articles include Basil Bernstein, "Social Structure, Language, and Learning," *Educational Research*, III (1961), 163–76, and by the same author, "Language and Social Class," *British Journal of Sociology*, XI (1960), 271–76. See also J. L. Fischer, "Social Influences on the Choice of a Linguistic Variant," *Word*, XIV (1958), 47–56. The relevance of social dialectology to teaching is explored in *Non-Standard Speech and the Teaching of English*, William Stewart, ed., (Washington D.C.: Center for Applied Linguistics, 1964). The social classes mentioned above are described in W. Lloyd Warner, *Social Class In America* (New York: Harper & Row, Publishers, 1960).

One of the best discussions of style in English is to be found in Porter Perrin, "The Varieties of English," pp. 1–40 in *Writer's Guide and Index to English* (Chicago: Scott, Foresman & Company, 1959). The division of styles into the range from intimate to ceremonial is based in part on Martin Joos, *The Five Clocks*, Publications of the Indiana University Research Center in Anthropology, Folklore, and Linguistics, Publication 22 (1962).

Some Concluding Remarks

CHAPTER 11 It would be possible to infer from most studies of the English language—including the preceding chapters—that the language consists of a group of unrelated subsystems: sounds, a grammar, a vocabulary, and the subsets from these which are related to nonlinguistic circumstances. Such an inference is almost totally incorrect. All the aspects of the English language form an integrated system; while we can all produce an infinite number of sentences, and while almost all of our sentences are unique, underlying them all can be discerned the set of rules which makes it possible for us to learn a language in the first place and in the second place to understand what our fellows say— including the unique things they say. All the parts of a language are interrelated, and their relation seems to be hierarchic. That is, deep and simple syntactic rules seem to underlie all of our sentences. These rules contain category terms which dominate subcategories; and the subcategories dominate the lexicon, which reflects a semantic system with implicit rules permitting and forbidding co-occurrence. The words which make up the lexicon have pronunciations. These in turn are affected by phonological rules that apply to the whole string of words, once they are assembled. Graphic, or spelling, rules are related to two other sets of rules—phonological ones and grammatical ones. And the dialects and other recognizable variant forms of English also involve not merely arbitrarily selected markers, but rather general drifts or tendencies—tendencies toward the loss of inflectional affixes, toward the simplification of consonant clusters, and the like.

The best language teaching materials will certainly be those which capitalize to the fullest extent on the interrelationships between the features of language. This means that school materials should be designed so that the most widely applicable—and the most basic—concepts are introduced first. Such concepts would certainly include the sentence, the notion of grammatical categories, and a fairly explicit definition of the terms "sound," "letter," and "word." Good language materials will also make explicit the relationships between the superficially unrelated aspects of language, such as spelling and grammatical analysis. Beginning reading, for example, should be so structured that it draws on the child's native command of the phonological, lexical, and syntactic systems of his language and relates these specifically to the printed material before him. The connections between the skills required for reading and those required for spelling are obvious; less obvious is the set of relationships between spelling and composition (for example, the fact that the processes of word building which account for the spelling of English complex words also relate to the achievement of focus and economy in sentence composition).

Thus in language study as in most other systematic disciplines, understanding the parts requires understanding the whole. The student who as his language study goes along develops a strong sense of the interrelatedness of all the aspects of language should acquire the kind of understanding that leads to language consciousness and control, regardless of the language task he is faced with. Of course, if the student is to understand the relevance of language to human social and artistic behavior he must be able to see language whole—to see the whole process of communication as basically the same kind of activity, a kind of activity parallel to other aspects of human behavior, and interrelated with all of them.

Ideally, it might seem, these objectives would best be realized by introducing a common linguistics into all school materials, from kindergarten through college. But this is obviously impossible; no full set of school materials reflecting a common theory of language even exists at the present time. And, more important, there is not at present anything like the kind of agreement among language theorists that there is among, say, chemists— the kind of agreement that permits teaching the same subject matter in approximately the same sequence wherever the subject is taught. But it is essential to remember that linguistics is not an "exact" science. In its present state of development it can be compared best to fields like psychology and economics, where there are indeed some common principles, but tremendous areas of disagreement. And linguistics is different from chemistry in another important way: its subject, language, is one which can be looked at profitably from several different points of view. Just as there are insights into the working of the human mind to be obtained from behaviorists, from Gestalt psychologists, from Freudians, and so on, despite the fundamental differences in their points of view, there are valid observations about language which result from rather different points of departure. Our approach has focused on language competence; but a grammar of performance is also possible, and it is, in fact, this kind of grammar which we seem to need if we are to relate language to external situations. That is, not just normalized deep-to-surface rules which produce sentences all speakers would call "grammatical," but also the false starts, the corrections, and the hesitation pauses have cultural implications, and these must seemingly be studied in a grammar of performance. Similarly, a grammar with a historical orientation provides insights not available in a purely synchronic grammar: irregularities in English spelling, for example, can be "explained" by general synchronic rules. They can also be explained by reference to history. Unpronounced letters and alternative spellings for the same sound sequences are the result of historical processes, and while from the point of view of the native speaker, the language has no history, from that of anyone trying to understand what language really is, history is of the utmost importance. The same thing can be said for various synchronic approaches to grammar. Some school systems introduce traditional grammar at one point in a student's career, structural at another, and some form of transformational-generative at still another. A strongly doctrinaire teacher may find it upsetting to have children entering his class who have an outlook on grammar—not to mention a vocabulary—which leaves them partially unprepared for what he hopes to teach. But if he is tolerant enough to be able to say something like "Now let's look at language in a different way," his students will gain something from the fact that they are allowed to look at language from different points of view. What is required of the teacher, particularly given the present state of research in linguistics, is some awareness of the various approaches to the study of language, some ability to translate from one to the other to the extent that translation is possible, and the ability to recognize the insights that each one offers. It is possible, provided teachers can adopt the attitudes just mentioned, for children to come out of a varied and even self-contradictory language program with better understanding of language than they would have had with a single approach.

For if one thing is certain it is that today's "linguistics"-oriented school materials are not the last word. The most famous series and the one most fully generative in approach reflects the linguistics of 1957. Most English language materials are still trying to assimilate the findings of the early 1950's, while others are frankly traditional. But a great deal has happened in linguistics during the past ten years to open up new areas of investigation and to develop new approaches rather than to produce solid findings. Thus the "new" linguistics materials available today are already old-fashioned, and within the next few years we can expect school language materials to contain subject matter hardly touched on in the past.

It is almost certain that the distinction between deep and surface structure, mentioned many times in the preceding chapters, will become an important part of school grammar, once there is more general agreement about exactly what is to be included in the deep grammar. It is equally certain that our whole notion of definition will be modified by the development of more fully specified dictionaries than have been imagined in the past. This development should make it easier to relate language study to both literature and social studies. Phonological studies which are just now coming out will also very likely revolutionize our teaching of sound systems, spelling, and punctuation. Instead of viewing surface structure as a sequence of sound segments with fixed stress patterns, we may need to look at it in the way suggested in the beginning of Chapter Six—as sound features with stress patterns reflecting the sequential or cyclic application of rules. Studies in the fields of psycholinguistics and sociolinguistics are also advancing rapidly, and it is almost certain that findings in these areas, particularly in the understanding of the process of language learning and in the way language growth and cultural experience must be interrelated will greatly influence the structure and content of language teaching materials.

Thus the teacher and the curriculum developer must face up to a very difficult task: they must provide students with a body of information about language sufficient to serve both their practical needs and their need for some understanding of language as a subject in itself. At the same time, they must provide a foundation in the study of language which will accept what may be a radically different technical vocabulary and theory of what language is and how it may be studied. Thus it is obvious that the child will benefit from being exposed to the contrasting approaches to language now available. It is also obvious that in linguistics as in other developing disciplines what is now available in school materials is already out of date. The objective of teaching thus must be not to make the students masters of a given linguistics dogma, but rather to make linguists of them. Not necessarily professionals, of course, but rather laymen who have had some experience in the investigation of language, who know what to look for, know something about how to look for it, and who have a vocabulary adequate to phrase the generalizations they come up with. They should be able to think and talk about language in other than purely impressionistic terms, and to frame their own generalizations both about language itself and about its relation to extralinguistic matters.

But if these are to be outcomes of language study, then the study can hardly be carried on in an authoritarian or dogmatic way. No one can argue that it is useless to know that certain words are called "nouns," others "verbs," and the like. But if language study is no more than learning a given set of category labels and producing lists of sentences according to the (necessarily limited) rules of a particular grammar, it can hardly lead to the outcomes discussed above. While the study of language competence must be deductive in the sense that it involves not the analysis of collections of data but rather the positing of rules which must be tested against data, it is not true that the role of the school is limited to imposing on the students a given set of rules. The objectives we have talked about depend on the student's participating in the formulation of hypotheses about his language. And despite the logical difficulties which an inductive approach involves (for example, finding a representative set of data when the total set is infinitely large), this approach may be best from the pedagogical point of view.

It is unrealistic, of course, to assume that the schools can devote large amounts of time to the study of language for its own sake. It seems impossible to shrug off the responsibility which the schools have traditionally been given to improve students' competence in something like "standard" English—

that is, a serious, public, written style. Furthermore, it may be possible for the schools to do some thing toward fostering the child's creativeness in language. This kind of ability will not be achieved by language analysis, by positing grammatical rules, by categorizing words and phrases, or by any other of the activities commonly called "grammar." The contribution grammatical study might make, however, is in encouraging a curiosity about language—dialect and stylistic variants, innovations, indirect uses of language, and the like—all of which ought to have the effect of freeing the child of some of his inhibitions and of encouraging innovation on his own part. And this kind of discovery must have as its frame of reference some awareness of the normal and predictable in language. Thus language inquiry, while not in itself training in creativity, provides a frame of reference for exploration of and experimentation in language innovation.

There is, of course, another aspect of the schools' responsibility in language teaching: that is to help children develop something like "taste," something beyond mere curiosity and innovation. There is no guarantee that a person with great language versatility, with the easy command of a great many ways of phrasing an idea (which might be encouraged by certain kinds of linguistic study) will have a sense of appropriateness. In achieving this objective, I think, it is hardly possible even to speculate about what the schools might encourage, beyond providing abundant experience in hearing and reading a wide range of successful examples of English. A prerequisite for developing this sense, however, must be confidence in one's ability to produce acceptable English. And this confidence comes not so much from successfully completing a series of lessons in good English as in having one's native English accepted. Any language program which leads to inhibition, to uncertainty, to an unwillingness to commit one's ideas to language is an unsuccessful program. It would appear that a prerequisite of a good language program would be that it give evidence of respect for all the varieties of English, that it build on, not destroy, the language the student already commands, that it increase, not limit, the range of language the student is master of. This suggests that language study must include the respectful study of regional and social varieties of English as well as of the various English styles. It also suggests that students should be encouraged to produce more than one kind of English, to write authentic conversations as well as authentic essays. Thus the role of linguistics in the development of language skill is not so much as the source of rules to be followed in producing standard English but rather as a framework for language inquiry. This inquiry involves both the features that characterize the grammatical utterances of all speakers, and also the features that mark potentially fascinating subsystems of English. If language study leads the student to interest in language itself and to a sense of competence in talking about language, then it has gone far toward realizing the practical goals which are its traditional justification.

Index

A

B

C

P

Palatal 81
Panini 12
Parallel construction 71
Part of speech 2, 14-15, 22, 28, 73
   alternation of 45
Participle 16, 37, 39, 71, 113
Particle 125
Passive transformation 36, 41, 52, 57-
   60, 63, 64, 113
Pedersen, Holger 11
Perfect 37
Perrin, Porter 145
Phoneme 77, 79, 80, 81, 83, 100
Phonetics 3, 77
Phonics 77, 92, 96, 99, 105
Phonological rules 146
Phrase structure rules 20
Pick, Anne 110
Pitt, Jack 75
Pivot 102
Polysyllable 90-92, 96, 101
Portmantcau 120
Postal, Paul M. 126
Postman, Leo 22
Postnominal modifier 16, 55-57, 67
Predicate 15, 23, 25, 29, 49
Pre-nominal 20
Preposition 15
Prepositional phrase 16, 56, 67
Prescriptive grammar 2-3, 4-5, 131
Process rules 26
Progressive aspect 36, 37
Pronoun 15, 25, 33-35
   interrogative 34
   personal 33, 35
   relative 34
Pro-verb 27
Pyles, Thomas 126

Q

Qualifier 41, 112
Question transformation 28, 29, 52-
   54, 66
Question word 41, 58-59

R

Reed, C. E. 145
Relative clause 52-60
Relative word 28, 56, 57, 58, 61, 67
Resonant 80
Restrictive clause 56, 57, 62-63
Rhetoric 65, 71, 118
Richards, I. A. 75
Rivers, Wilga M. 75
Roberts, Paul 17, 22, 50, 68, 76
Robertson, Stuart 126
Rogers, Will 124
Rosenbaum, Peter 22, 51, 60, 67

S

Sapir, Edward 11
Sebeok, Thomas A. 126
Secondary meanings 120
Segmentation of sounds 80
Semantic feature 115-117
Semivowel 87
Sense verb 50
Sentence 8, 15-16, 23-25, 49
   completeness 24, 49
   complex 15, 16, 20, 30, 64-65, 66, 71
   compound 16, 64-65, 66
   declarative 16
   exclamatory 16
   imperative 16, 36, 49, 67
   in Noun Phrase 29, 31-32
   interrogative 16
   punctuation 24
   simple 15, 18, 20, 64-65, 66
Sentence modifier 65
Shakespeare, William 121, 127, 129
"Shall"-"will" rules 4
Shaw, G. B. 87
Short vowel 83, 84, 85, 99, 102-103
Shuy, Roger 98
Silent *e* 103
Simile 118
Slager, William R. 76
Sledd, James 17
Smith, Henry Lee 98
Sound-letter correspondence 93, 101
Sound symbolism 10
Staal, J. F. 67